MILLAIS'S ILLUSTRATIONS

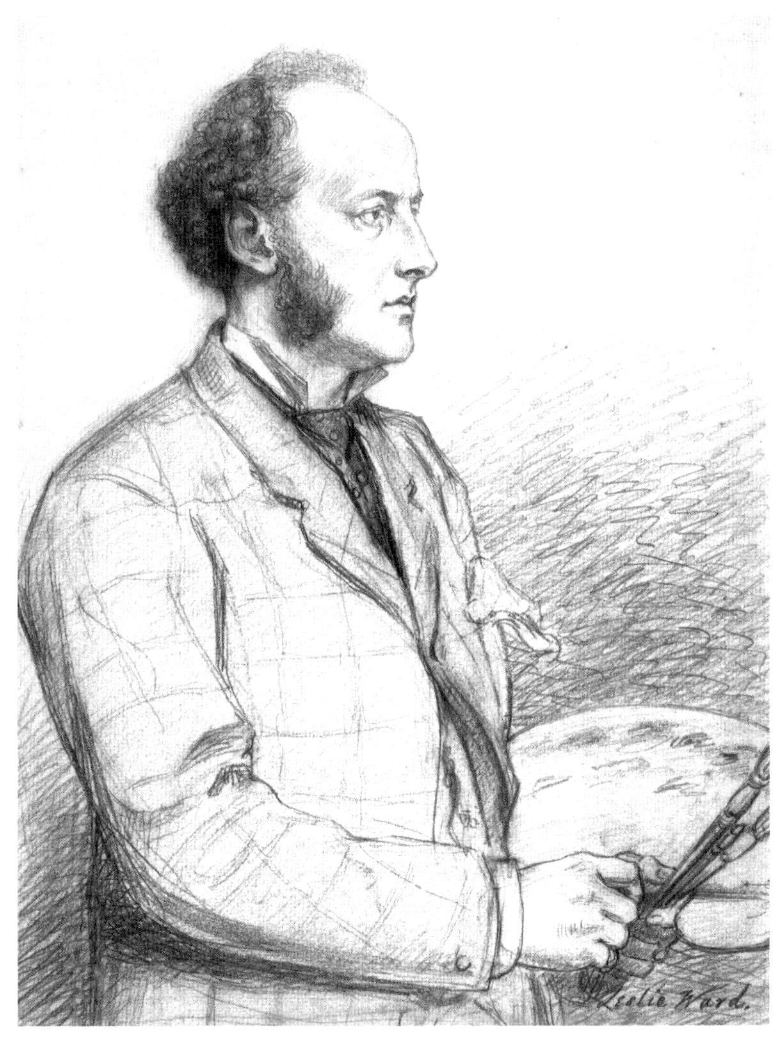

John Everett Millais by Leslie Ward ('Spy'), 1874,
pencil drawing subsequently used for
a wood engraving

MILLAIS'S ILLUSTRATIONS

A Collection of Drawings on Wood

BY

JOHN EVERETT MILLAIS, R.A

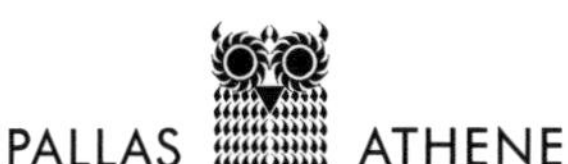
PALLAS ATHENE

LIST OF THE COLLECTION.

NO.	SUBJECT.	ORIGINALLY PUBLISHED IN
1	The Finding of Moses	*Lays of the Holy Land*
2	The Grandmother's Apology	*Once a Week*
3	Margaret Wilson, the Scottish Martyr	*Once a Week*
4	On the Water	*Once a Week*
5	A Scene in Merrie England	*Once a Week*
6	No Surrender	*Orley Farm*
7	"The Wind is blowing in Turret and Tree"	*Poems by Alfred Tennyson*
8	"There's nae Luck about the House"	*The Home Affections*
9	"Bitterly Weeping I Turned Away"	*Poems by Alfred Tennyson*
10	Herr Willy Koenig	*Papers for Thoughtful Girls*
11	The Revival	*Poems by Alfred Tennyson*
12	Hilary's Resolution	*Good Words*
13	In the Churchyard	*Good Words*
14	Mary Queen of Scots at Buxton	*Once a Week*
15	Farewell	*Orley Farm*
16	The Head of Bran	*Once a Week*
17	Prince Philibert	*Good Words*
18	"Watching their Idol as he Galloped Away"	*Once a Week*
19	"Toll ye the Church Bell"	*Poems by Alfred Tennyson*
20	La Fille bien gardée	*Once a Week*
21	Our Sister Grizel	*Papers for Thoughtful Girls*
22	"Bring the dress and put it on her / That she wore when she was wed"	*Poems by Alfred Tennyson*
23	Von Bauhr's Dream	*Orley Farm*
24	Sorrow in the Heart	*Orley Farm*
25	"Let us speak together before we sleep"	*Once a Week*
26	Ciss Berry's Arrival	*Papers for Thoughtful Girls*
27	Dark Gordon's Bride	*Once a Week*
28	"I am aweary, aweary!"	*Poems by Alfred Tennyson*
29	The Plague of Elliant	*Once a Week*
30	Polly	*Good Words*
31	Lady Carew and Margaret	*Once a Week*
32	Christmas at Noningsby—Morning	*Orley Farm*
33	The Sleeping Palace	*Poems by Alfred Tennyson*
34	"I'll win the Key from My Father's side"	*Once a Week*
35	The Fair Jacobite	*Once a Week*
36	Dame Dorothy	*Papers for Thoughtful Girls*
37	"Oh the Lark is Singing in the Sky"	*Good Words*
38	The Unjust Judge	*Good Words*
39	In the Boot Shop	*Good Words*
40	"And how are they all at Noningsby?"	*Orley Farm*
41	The Mite of Dorcas	*Once a Week*
42	St. Bartholomew	*Once a Week*
43	Mrs. Ascott's Death-bed	*Good Words*

LIST OF THE COLLECTION.

NO.	SUBJECT.	ORIGINALLY PUBLISHED IN
44	ANNA AND HER LOVER	*Once a Week*
45	THE PRAYER OF THE THIRTY TO ST. KADO	*Once a Week*
46	FOOTSTEPS IN THE CORRIDOR	*Orley Farm*
47	JOHN KENNEDY AND MIRIAM DOCKWRAITH	*Orley Farm*
48	"YET FILL MY GLASS; GIVE ME ONE KISS" . . .	*Poems by Alfred Tennyson*
49	LADY STAVELY INTERRUPTING HER SON AND SOPHIA FARNWAL.	*Orley Farm*
50	"DREW FORTH THE POISON WITH HER BALMY BREATH" .	*Poems by Alfred Tennyson*
51	SORTING THE PREY	*Once a Week*
52	"ANNA RESTED ON HER HOE AND LISTENED" . . .	*Once a Week*
53	"PREACHING DOWN A DAUGHTER'S HEART"	*Poems by Alfred Tennyson*
54	THE TEN VIRGINS	*Good Words*
55	"THE WORD SHE SPAKE SO SOFT AND LOW A BIRD HATH TA'EN TO DANDELOT"	*Good Words*
56	ORLEY FARM	*Orley Farm*
57	THE MILLER'S DAUGHTER	*Poems by Alfred Tennyson*
58	MISS HILARY'S PUPIL	*Good Words*
59	THE MEETING	*Once a Week*
60	THE WEDDING MORNING	*Good Words*
61	WATCHING	*Unpublished*
62	CHRISTMAS AT NONINGSBY—EVENING	*Orley Farm*
63	CLEOPATRA	*Poems by Alfred Tennyson*
64	A VISITOR ANNOUNCED	*Good Words*
65	"GUILTY"	*Orley Farm*
66	THE MONK	*Once a Week*
67	WAITING IN THE RAILWAY STATION	*Good Words*
68	MAUDE CLARE	*Once a Week*
69	"ONLY A SERVANT"	*Good Words*
70	"MANY AN EVENING BY THE WATERS DID WE WATCH THE STATELY SHIPS, AND OUR SPIRITS RUSH'D TOGETHER AT THE TOUCHING OF THE LIPS"	*Poems by Alfred Tennyson*
71	ELIZABETH HAND'S FIRST PLACE	*Good Words*
72	LOVE	*Poets of the Nineteenth Century*
73	LADY MASON AFTER HER CONFESSION	*Orley Farm*
74	FARMER CHELL'S KITCHEN	*Once a Week*
75	"'NEVER' IS A VERY LONG WORD"	*Orley Farm*
76	DOING ROYAL ERRANDS IN MERRIE ENGLAND	*Once a Week*
77	LADY MASON GOING BEFORE THE MAGISTRATE . . .	*Orley Farm*
78	"BOTH WERE YOUNG AND ONE WAS BEAUTIFUL" . . .	*Poets of the Nineteenth Century*
79	PICK-A-PACK	*Unpublished*
80	FAREWELL	*Orley Farm*

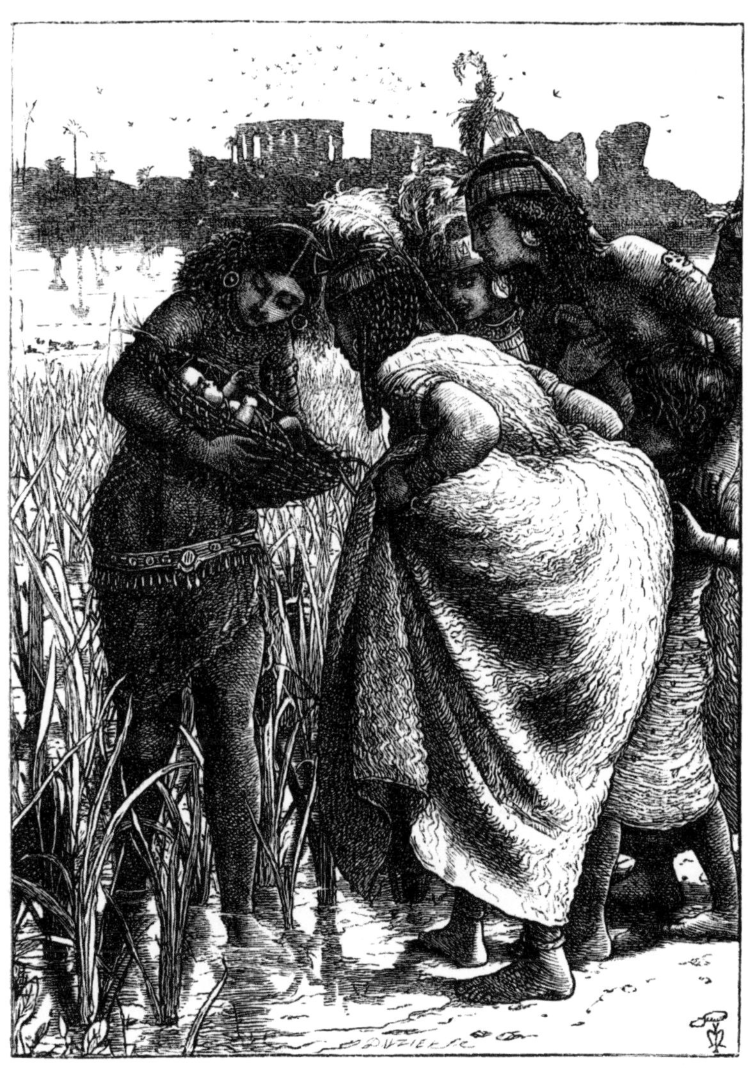

I

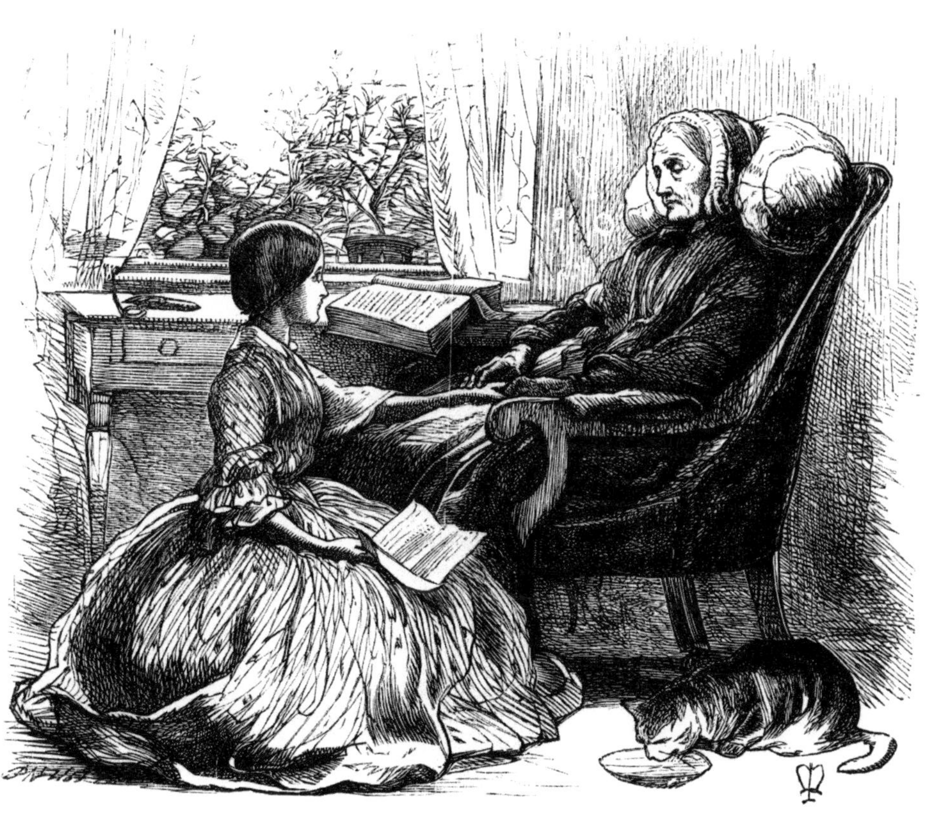

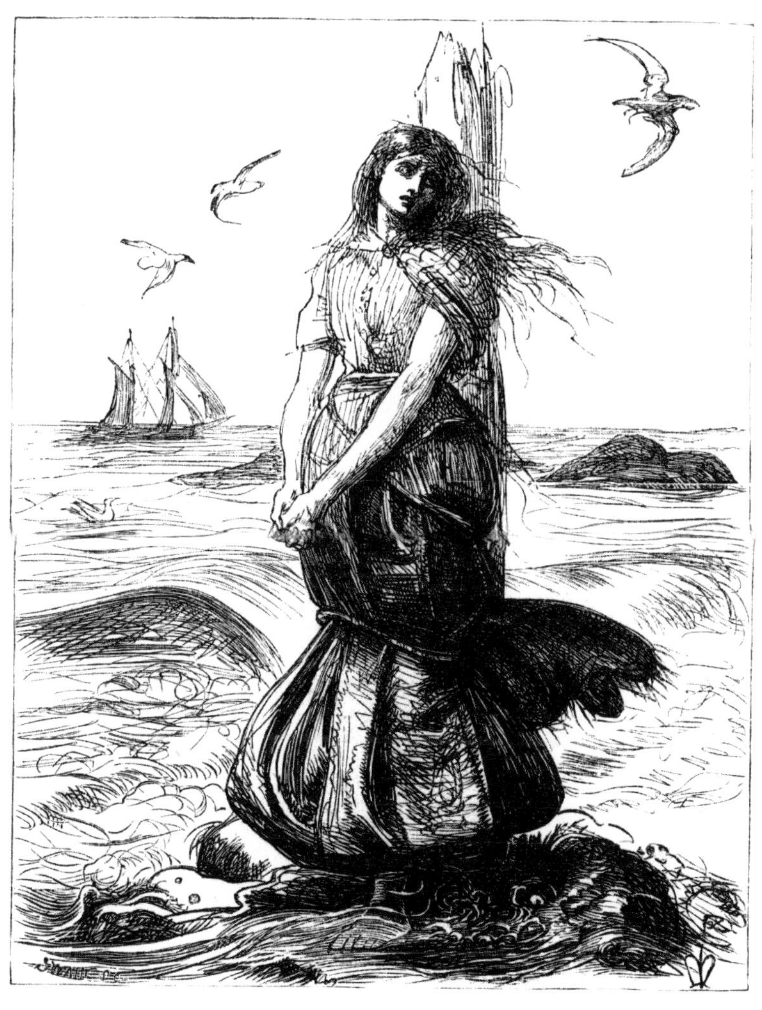

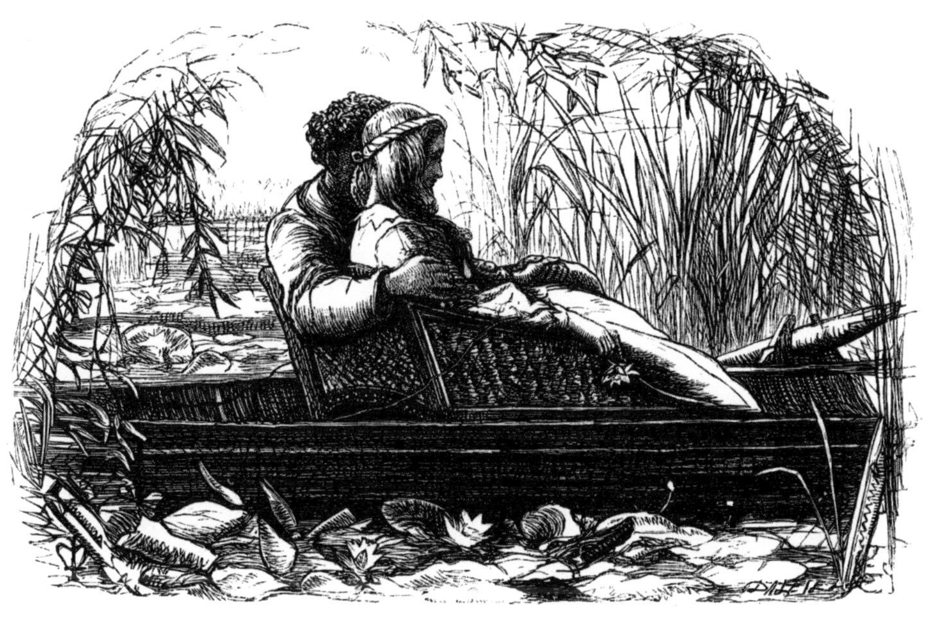

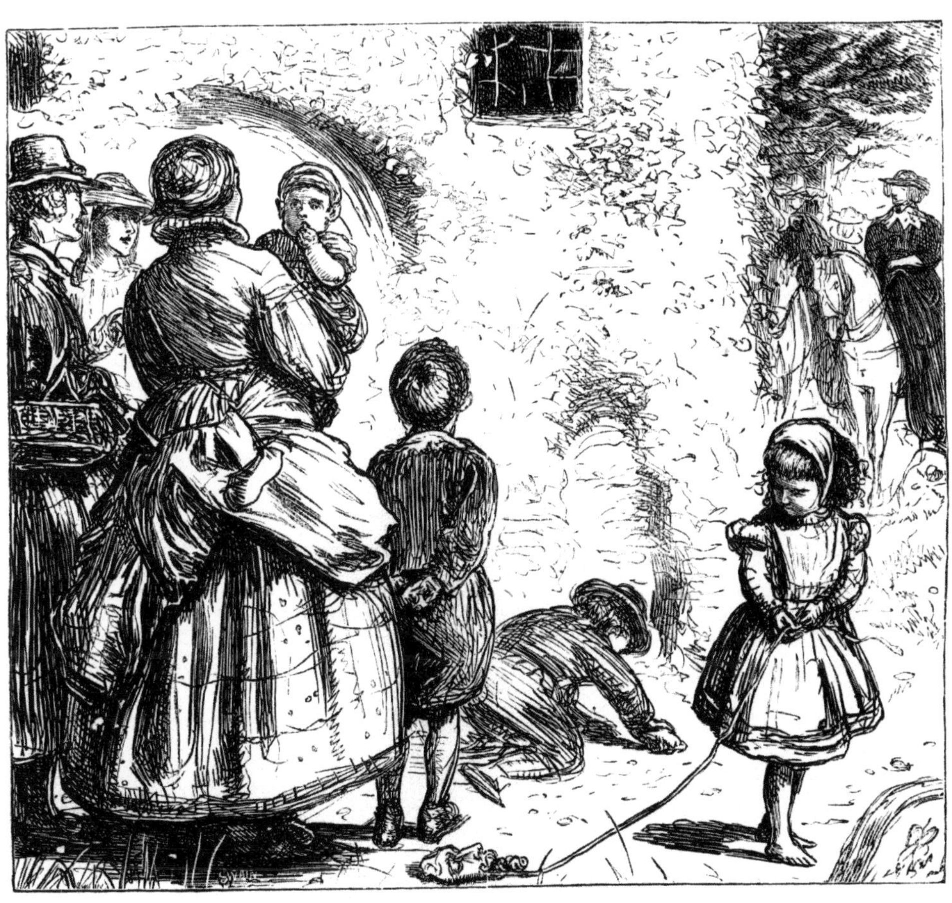

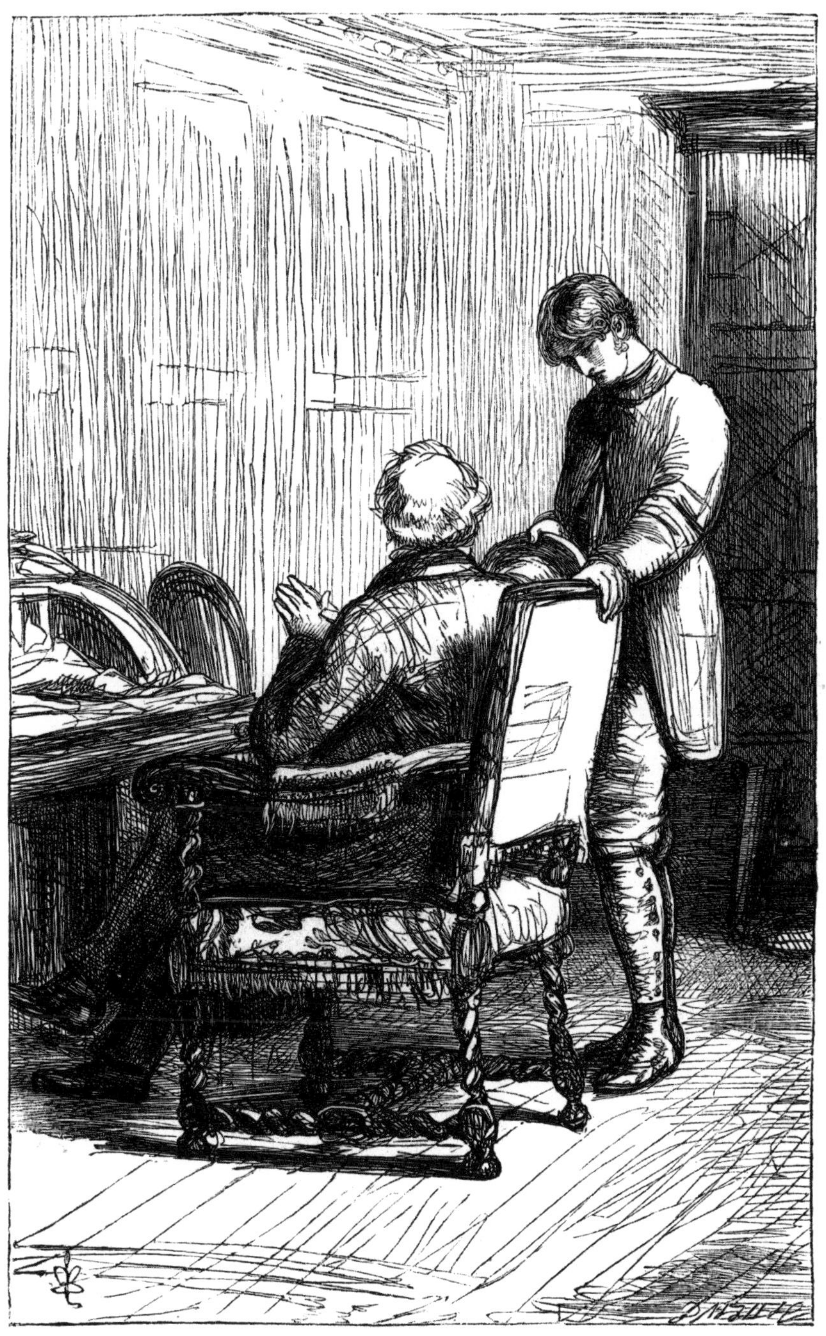

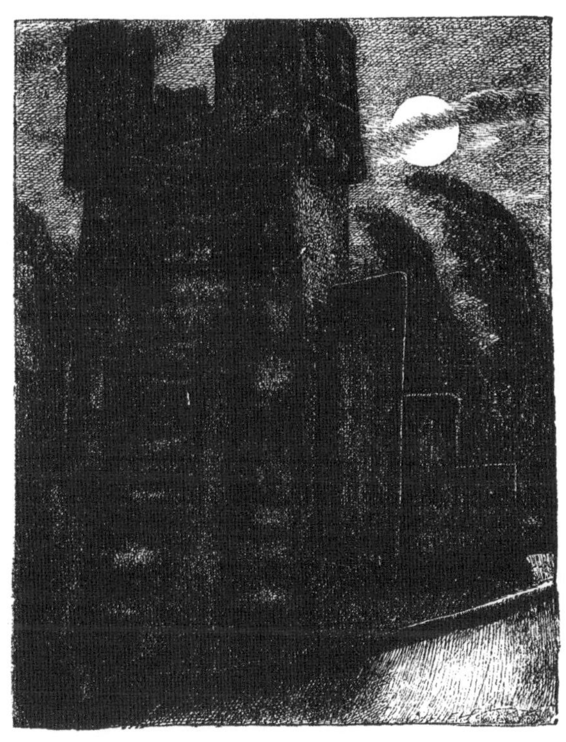

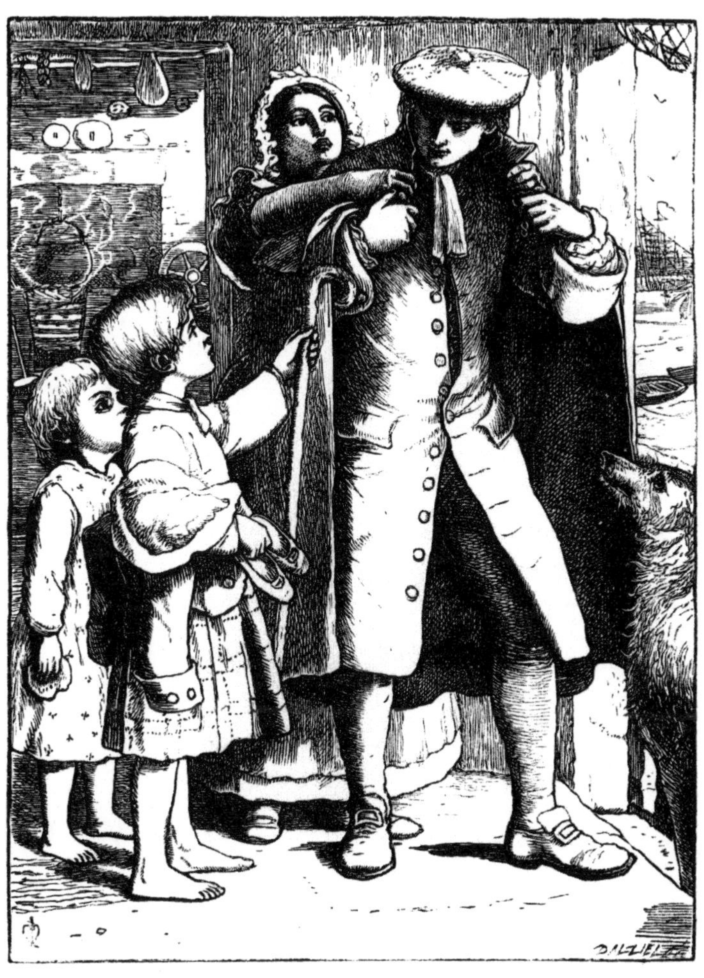
DALZIEL

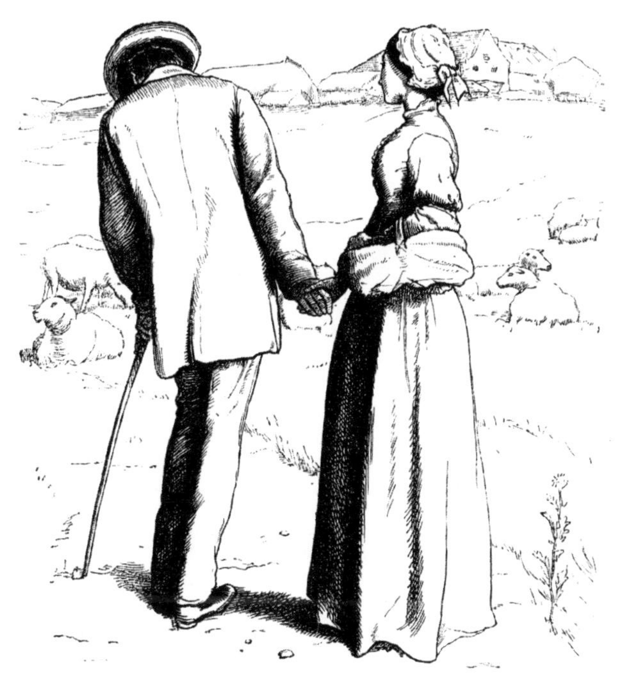

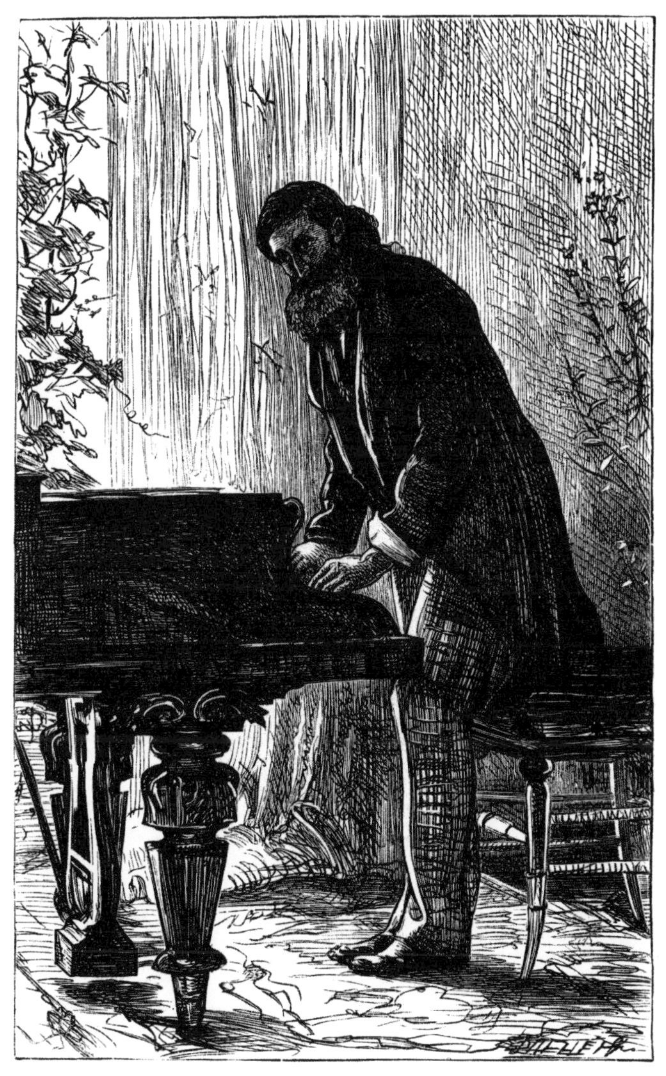

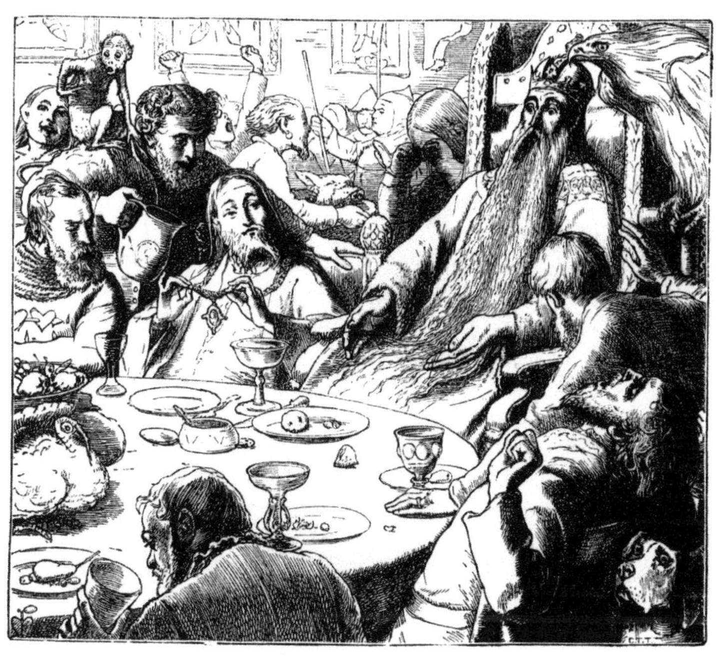

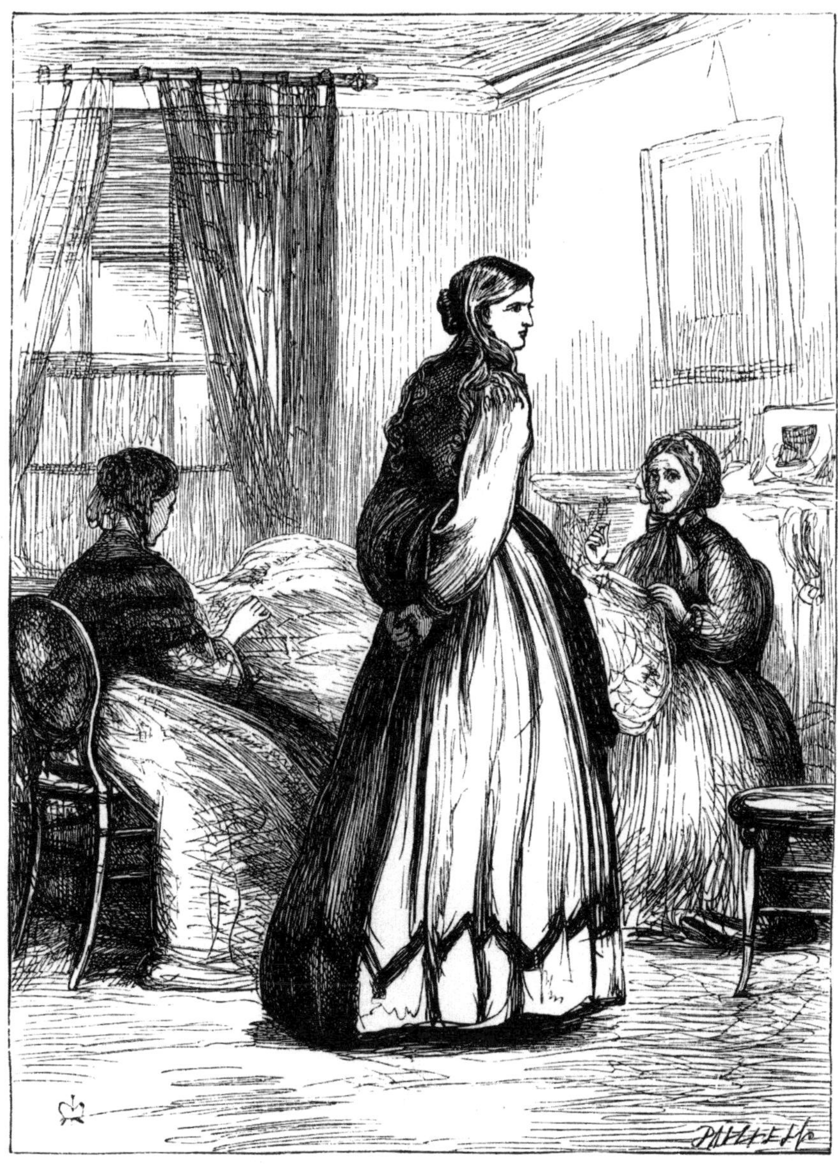

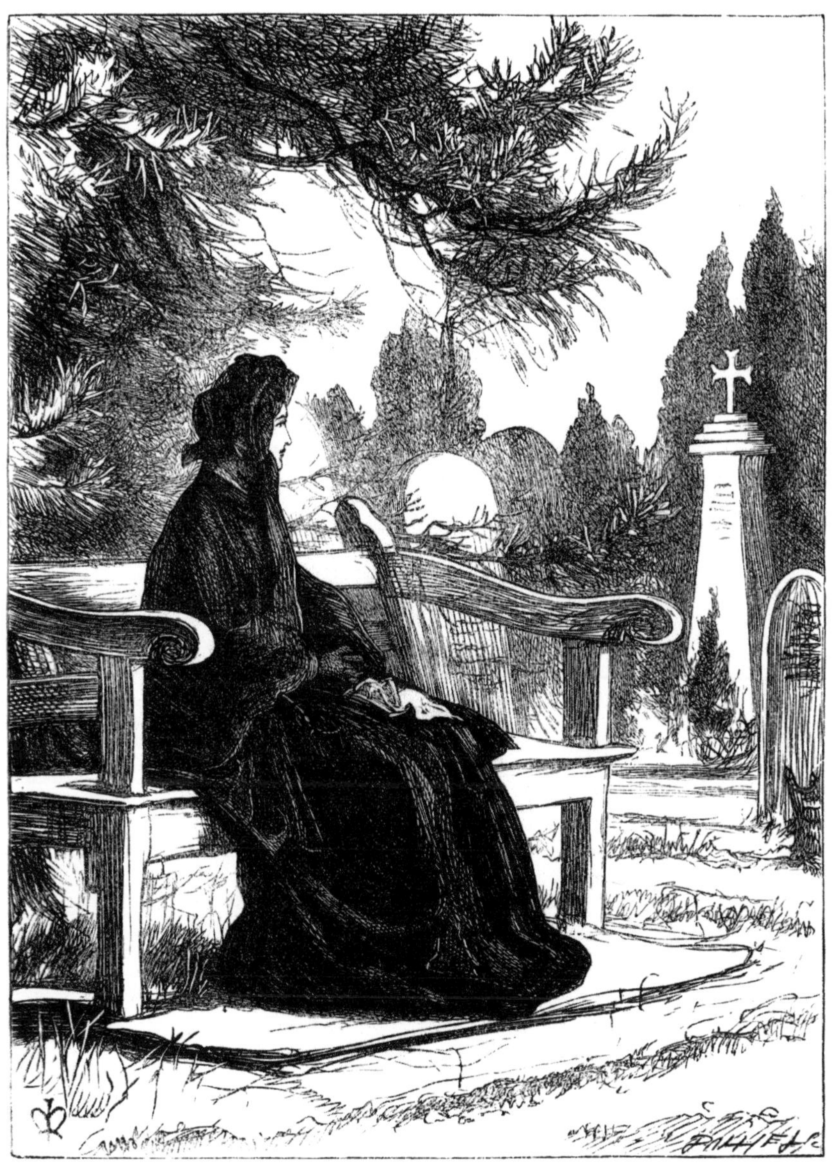

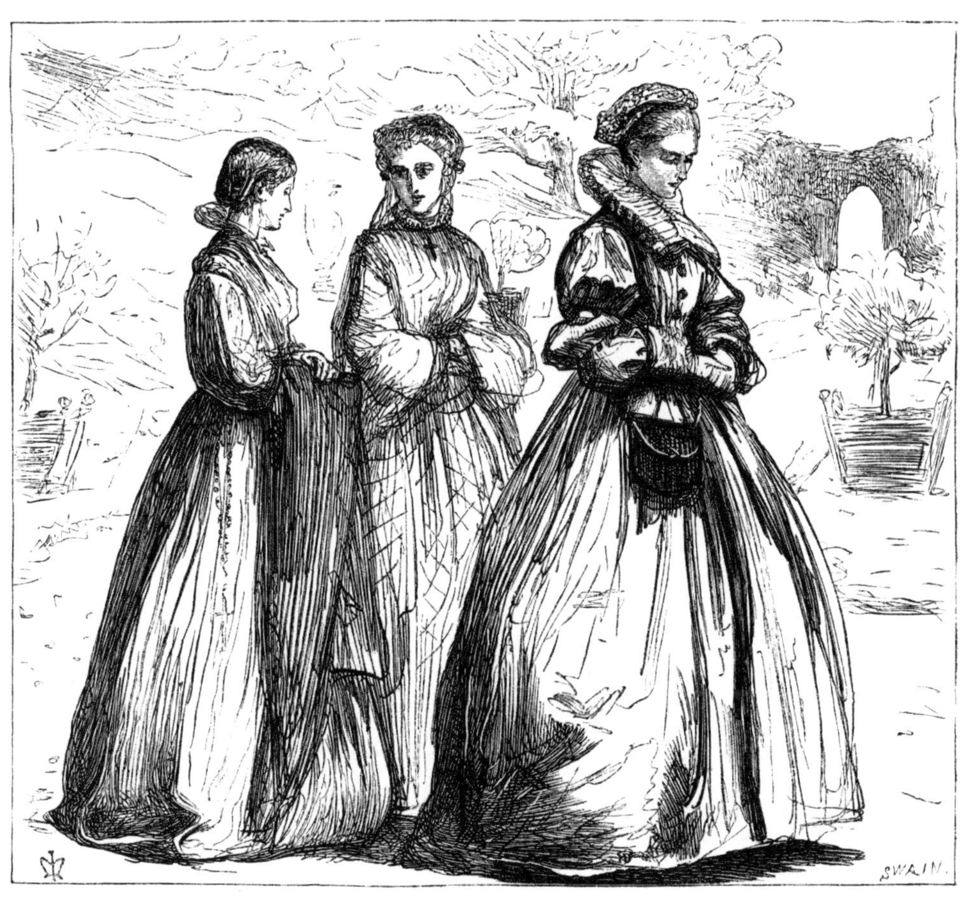
SWAIN.

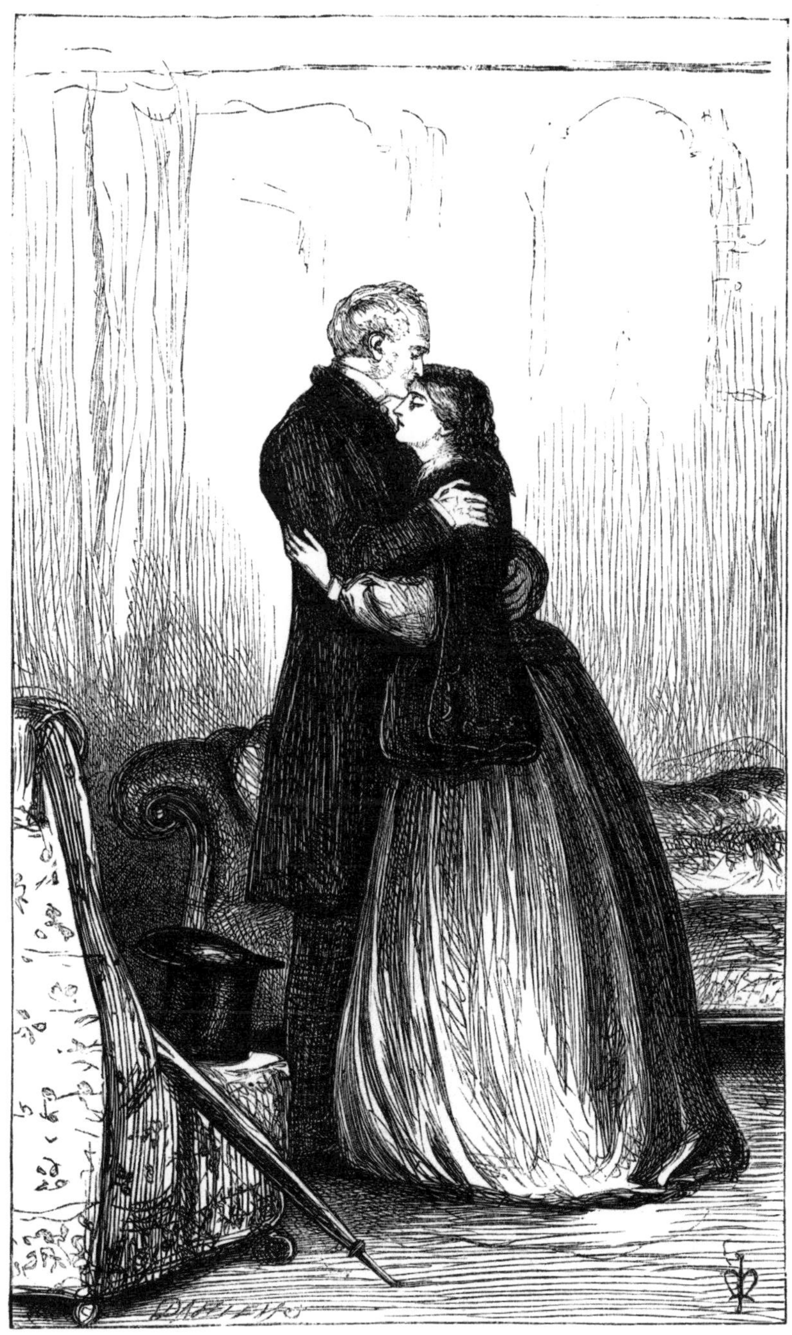

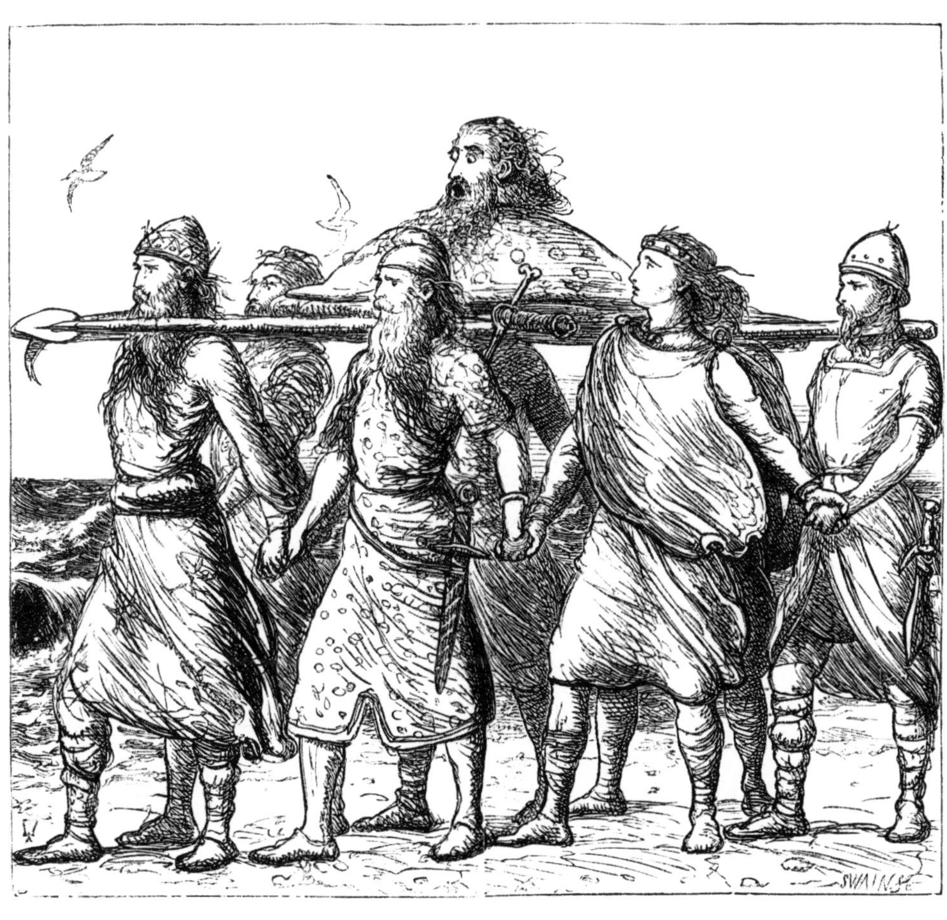
SWAIN SC

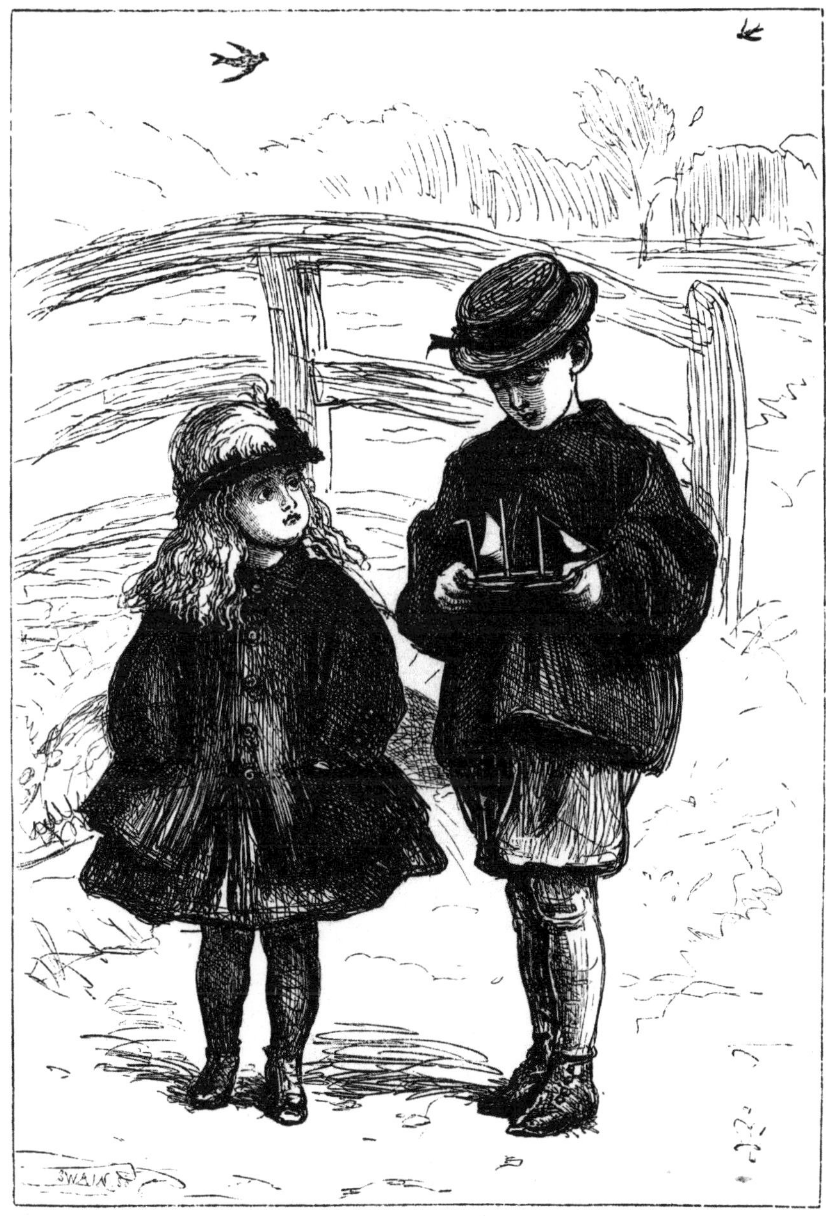
SWAIN

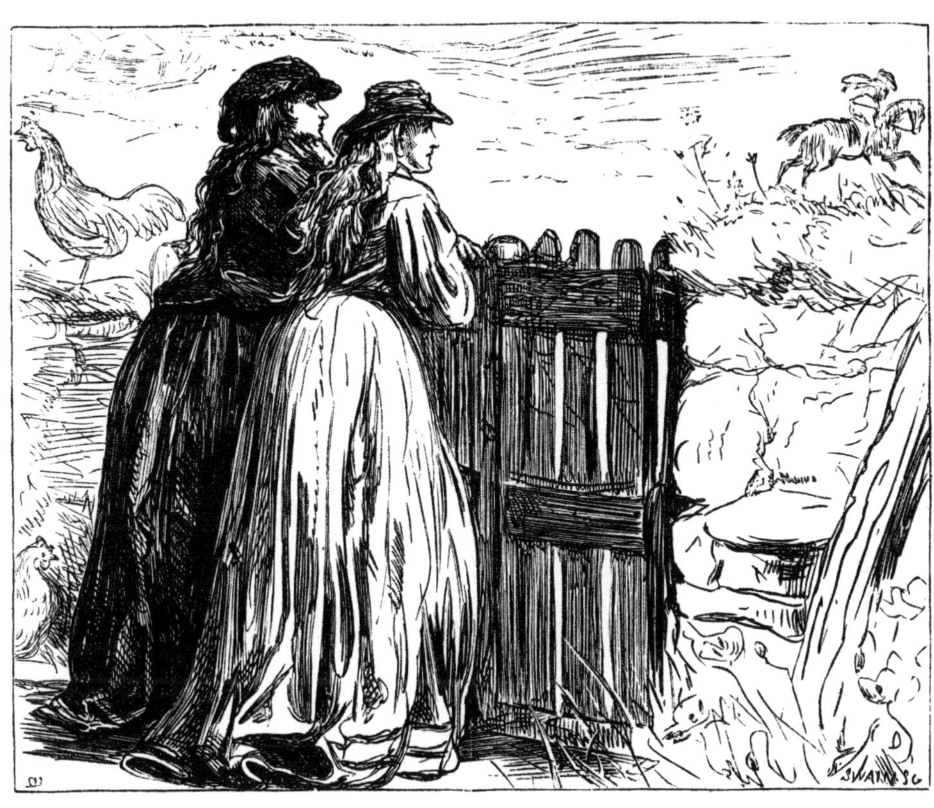

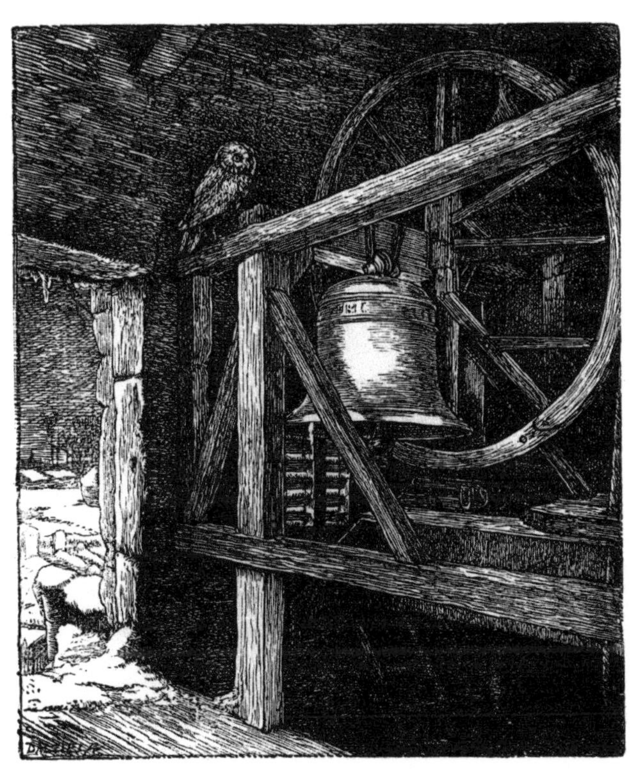

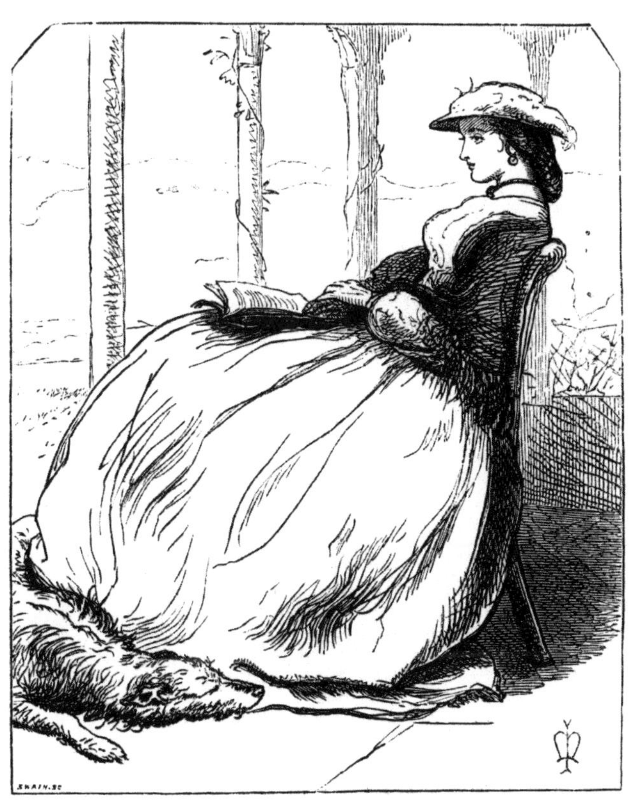
SWAIN. SC

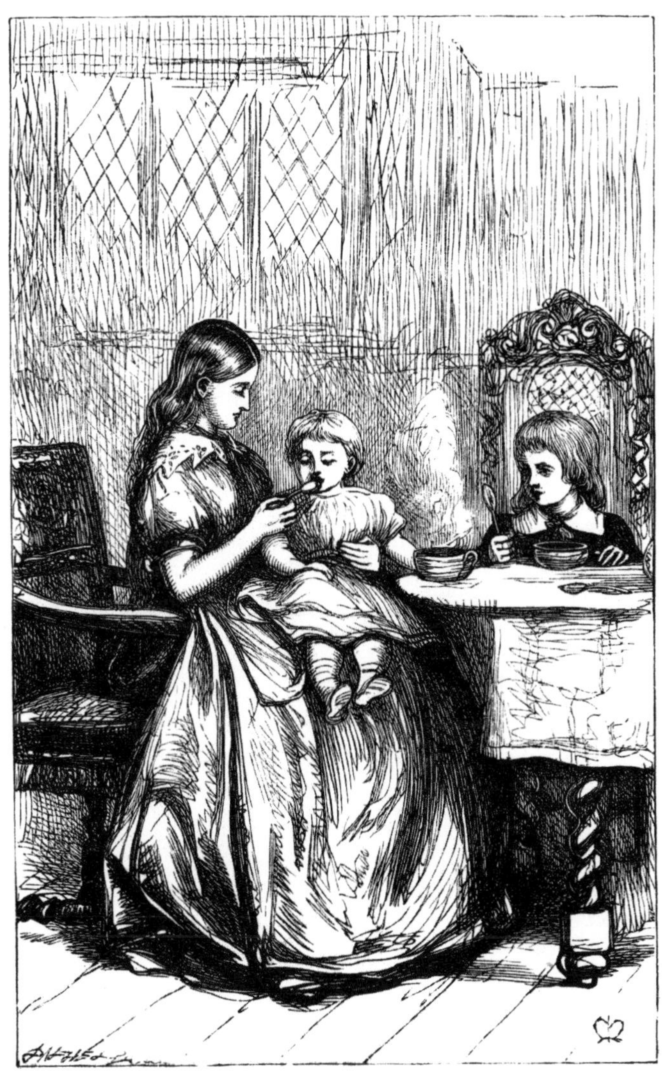

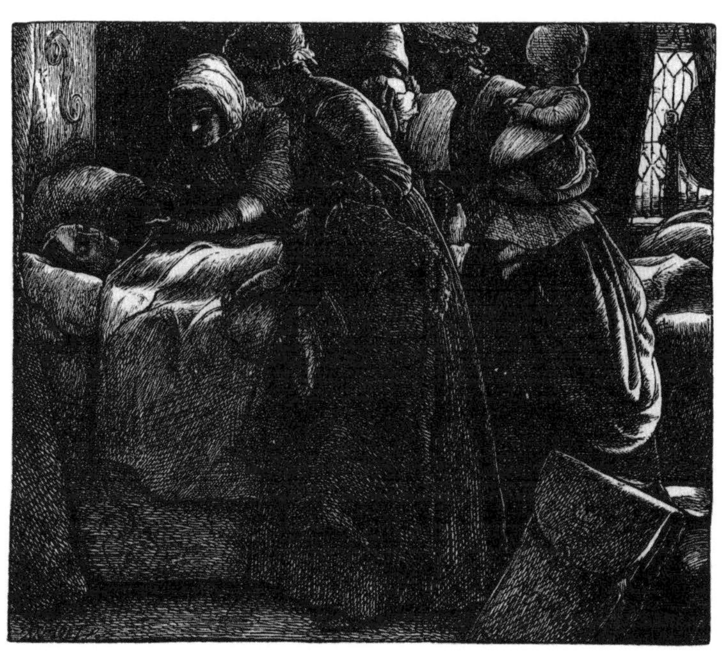

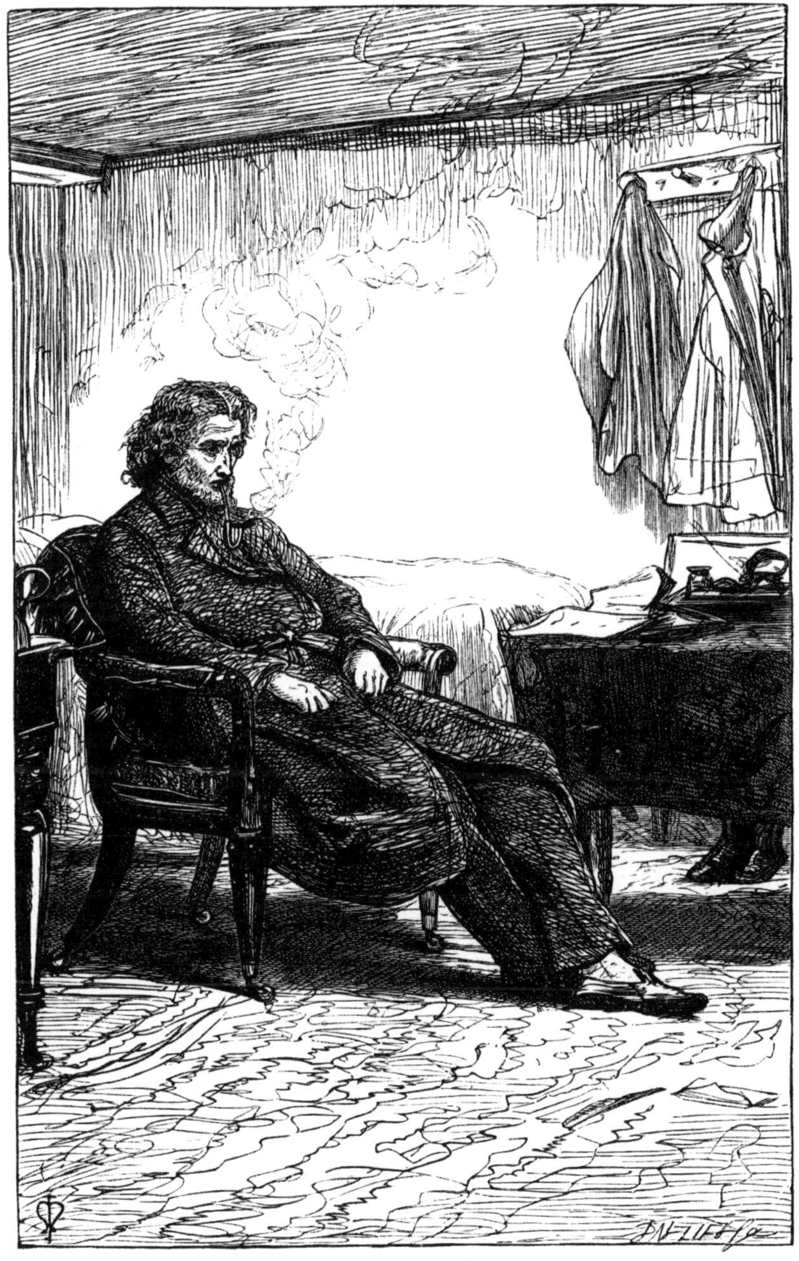

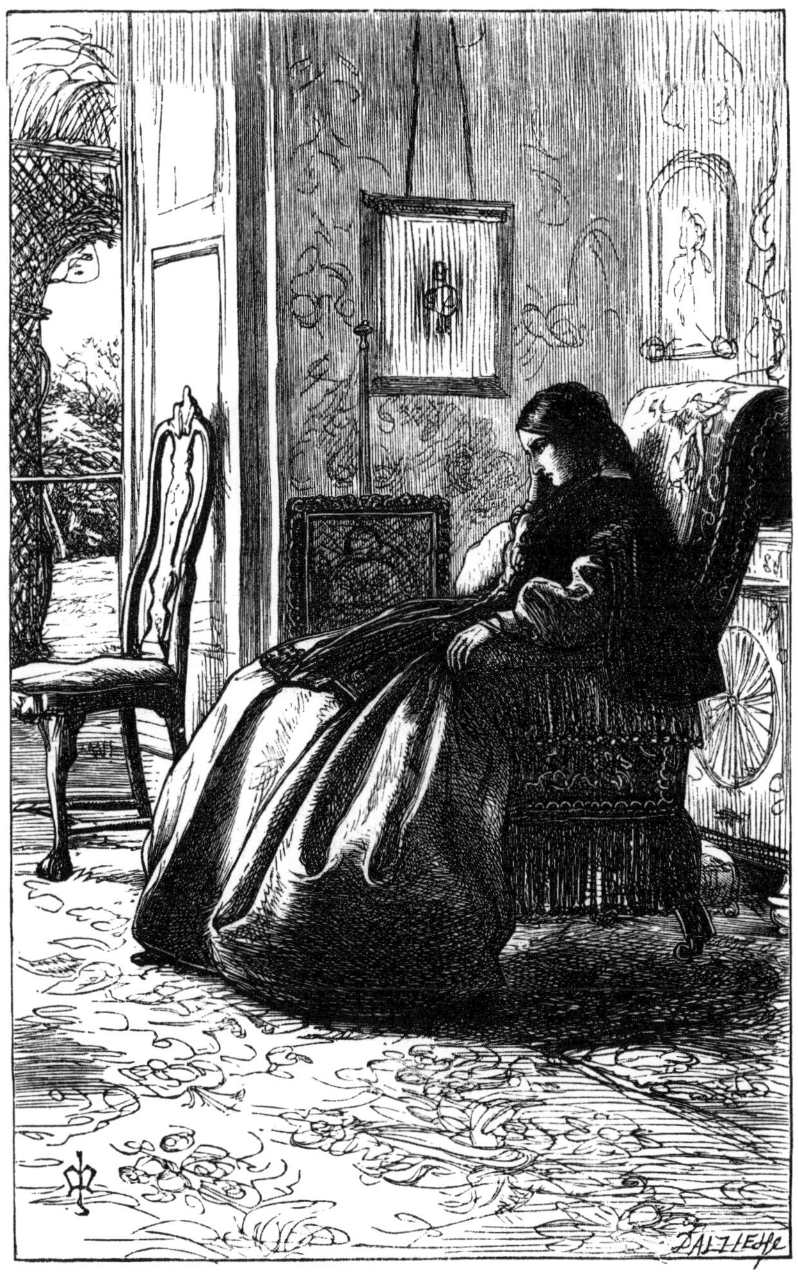
DALZIEL Sc

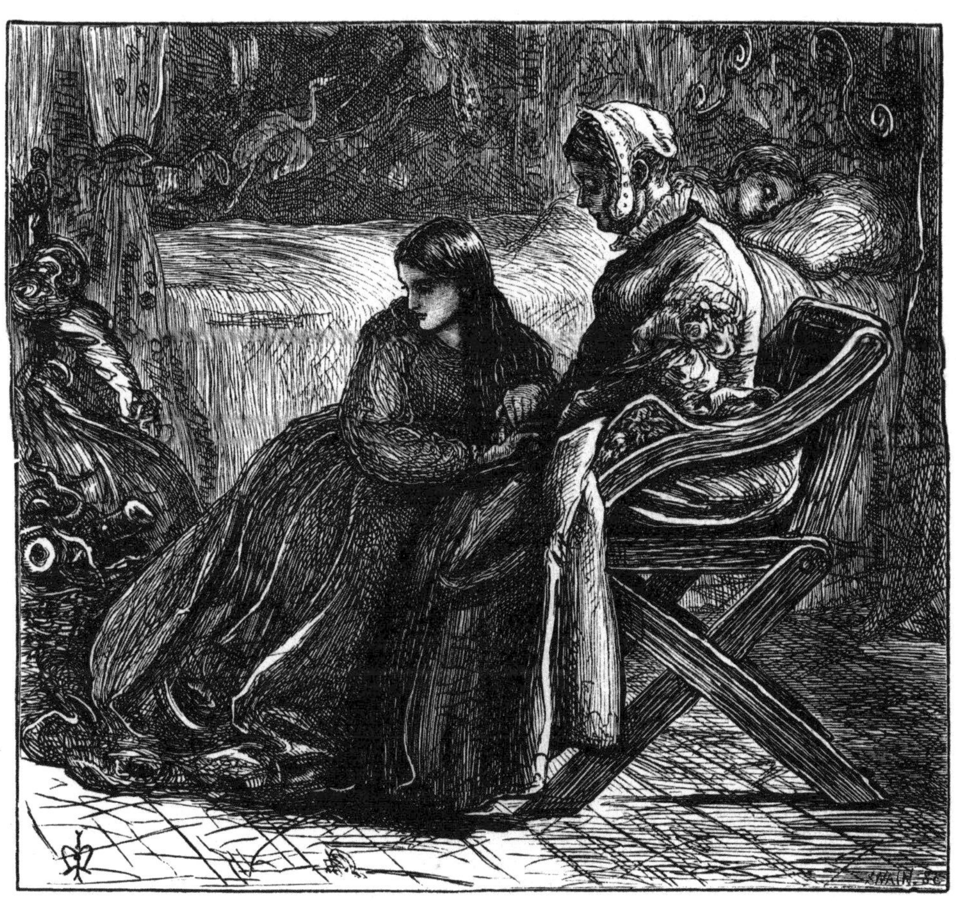

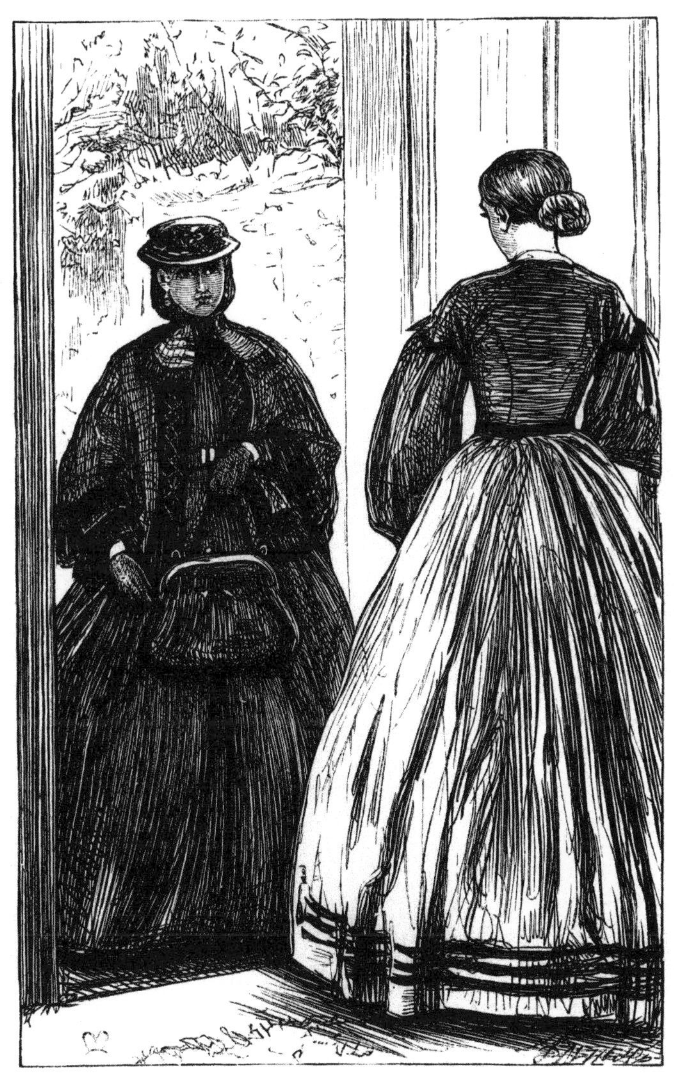

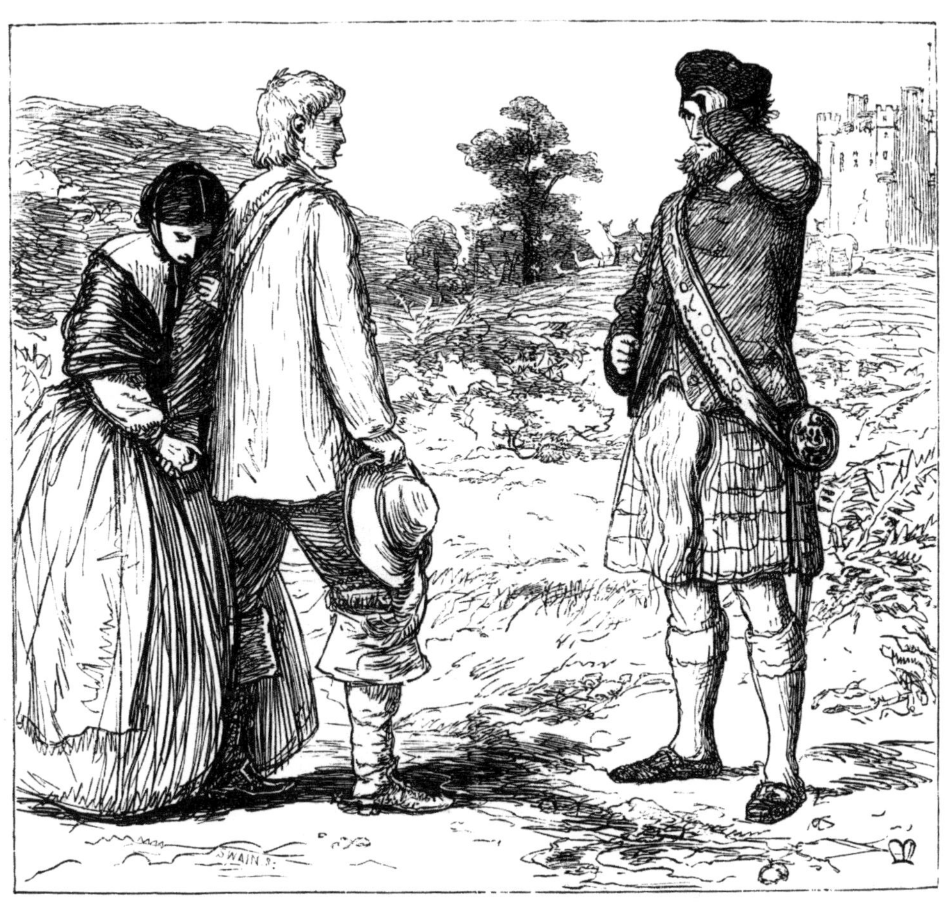
SWAIN

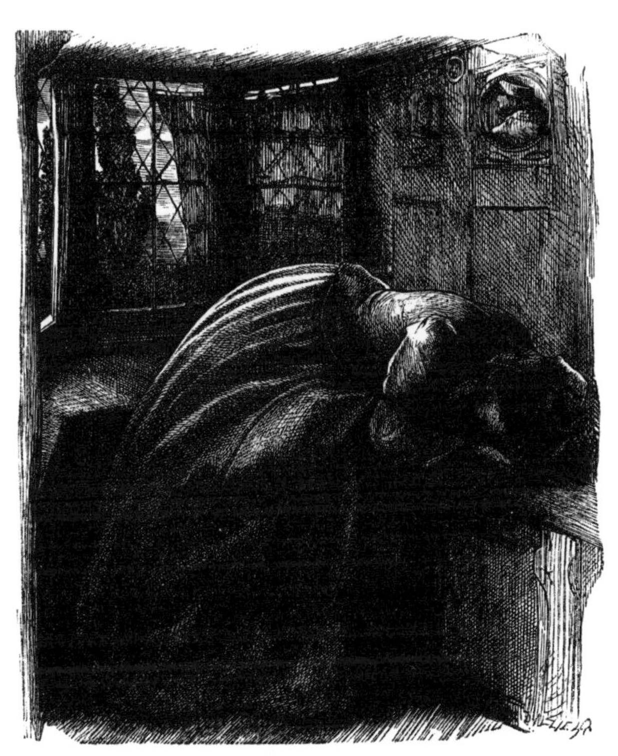

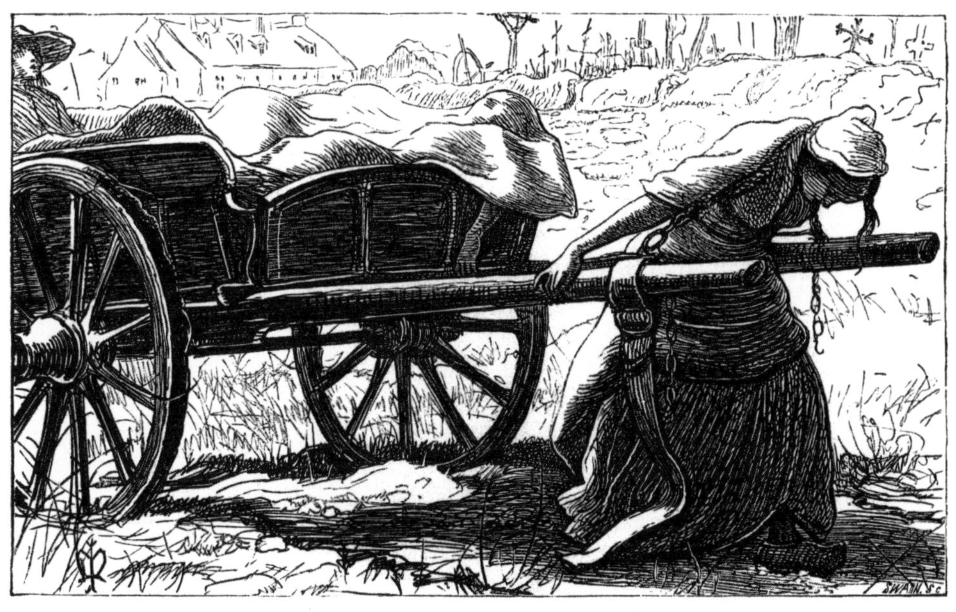
SWAIN. Sc

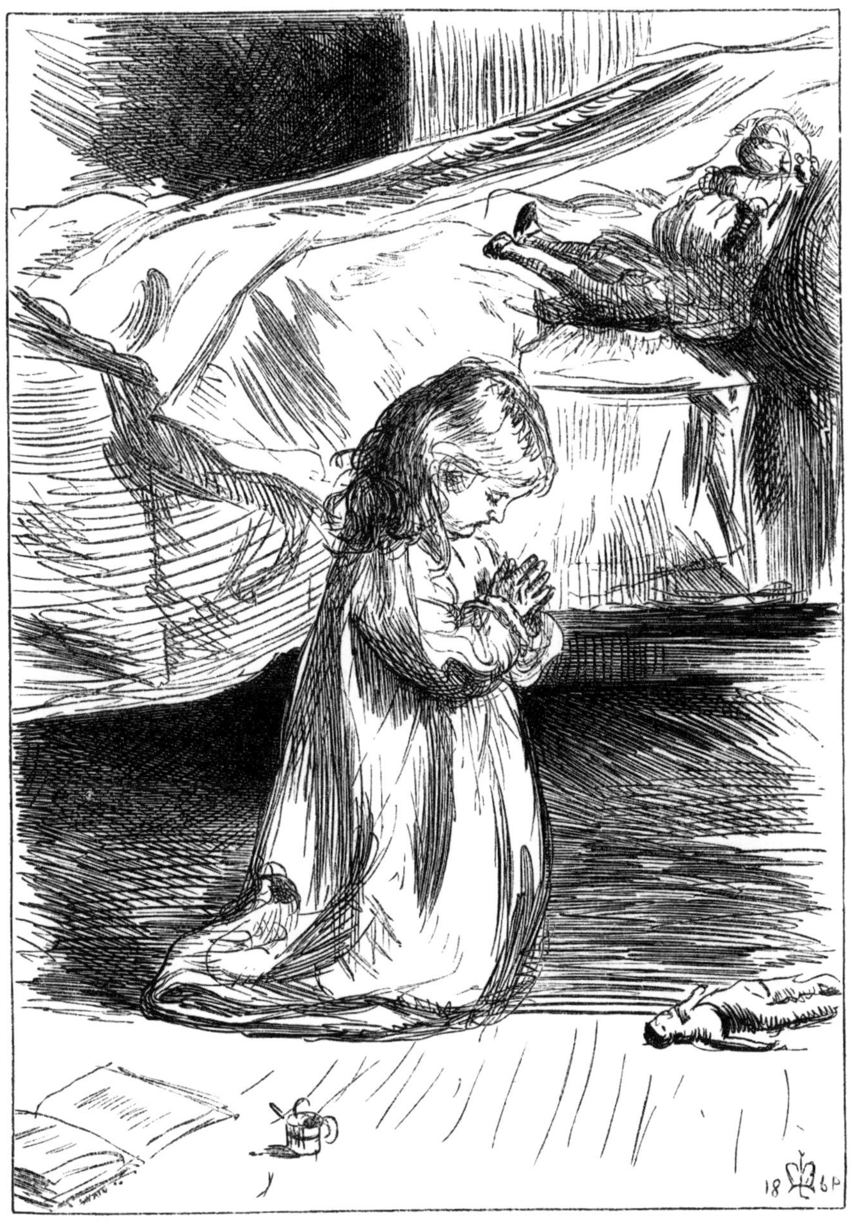

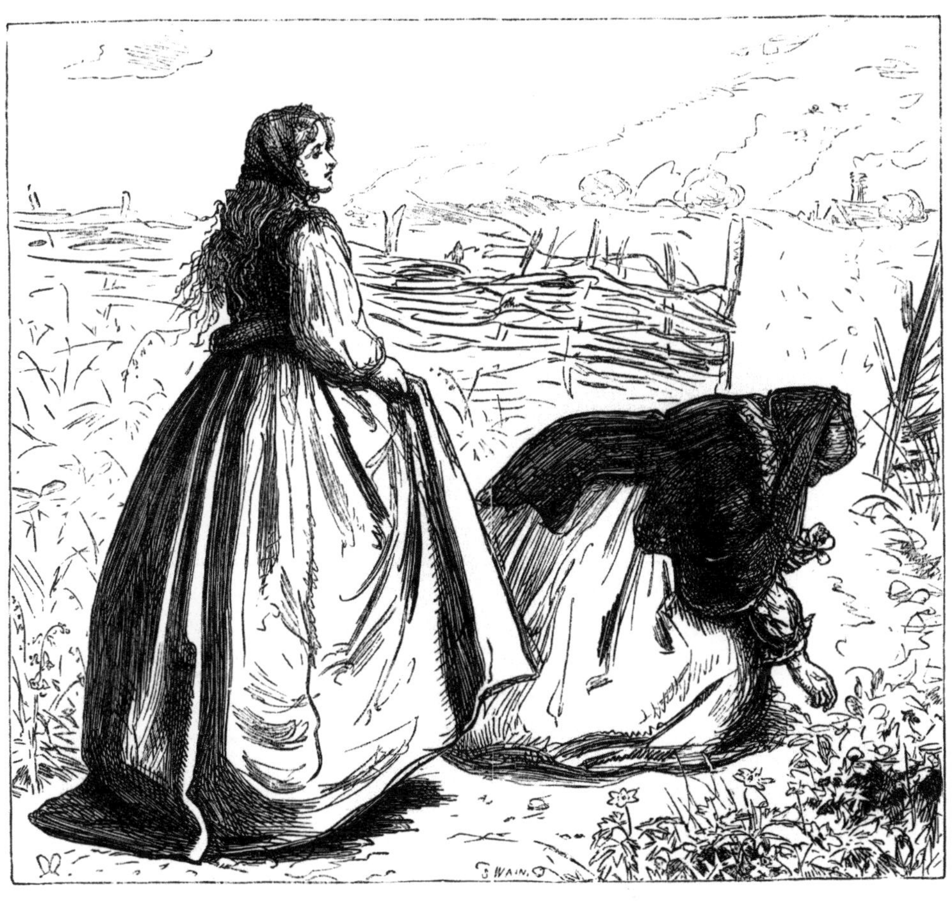
SWAIN

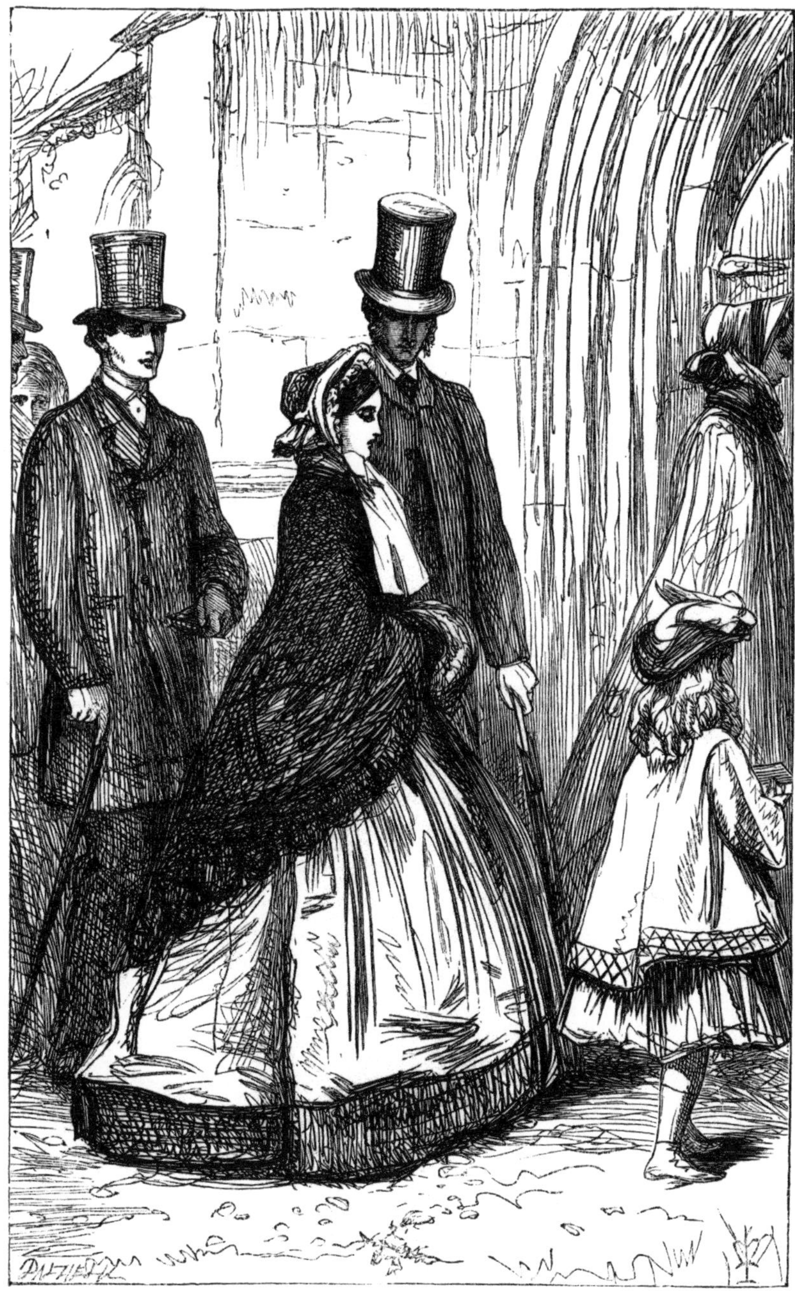

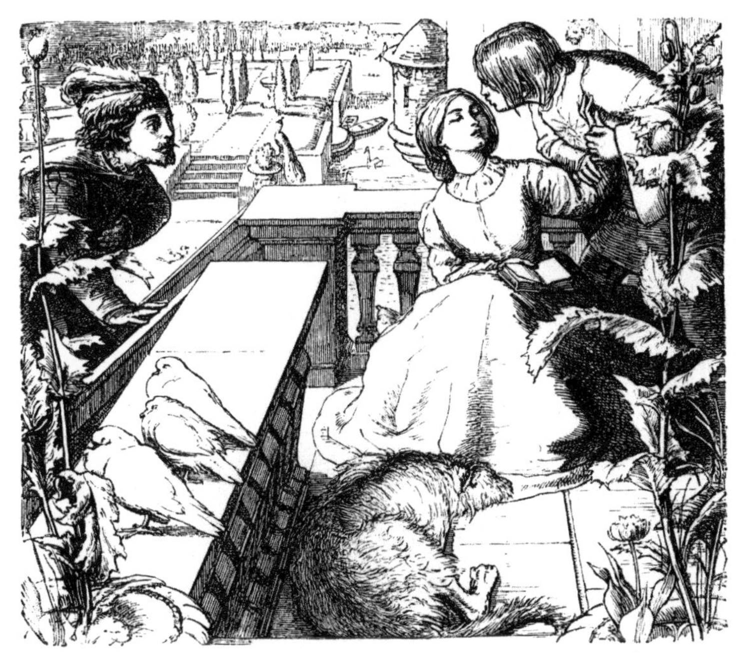

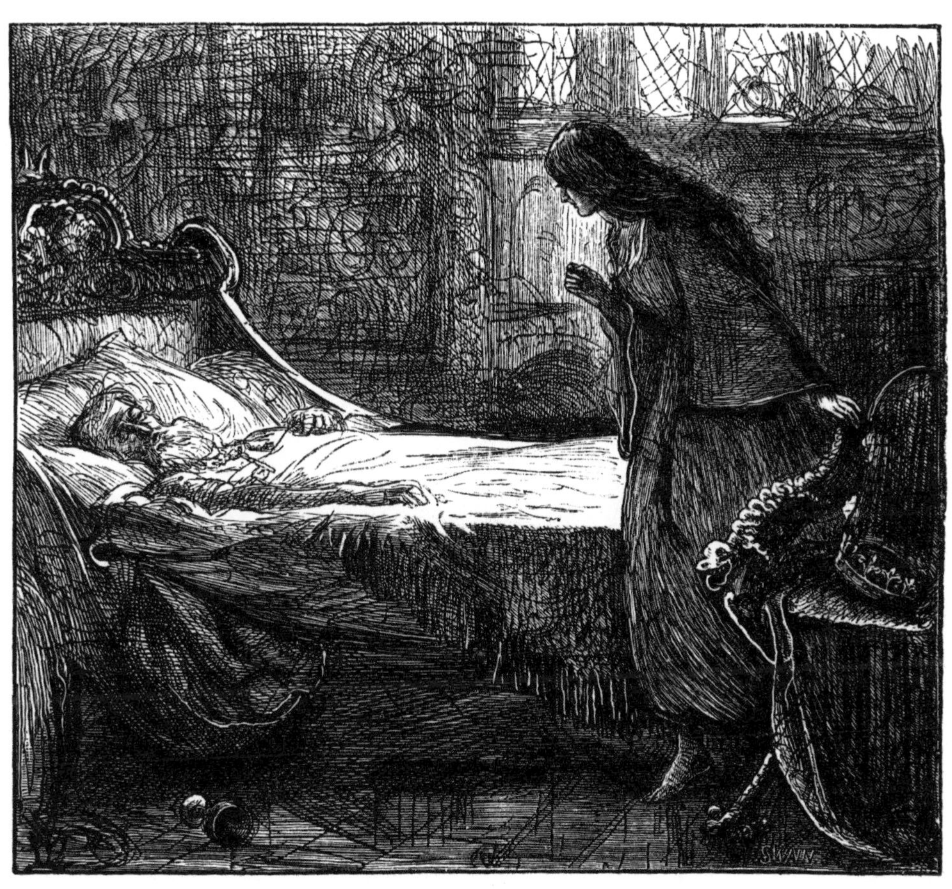
SWAIN

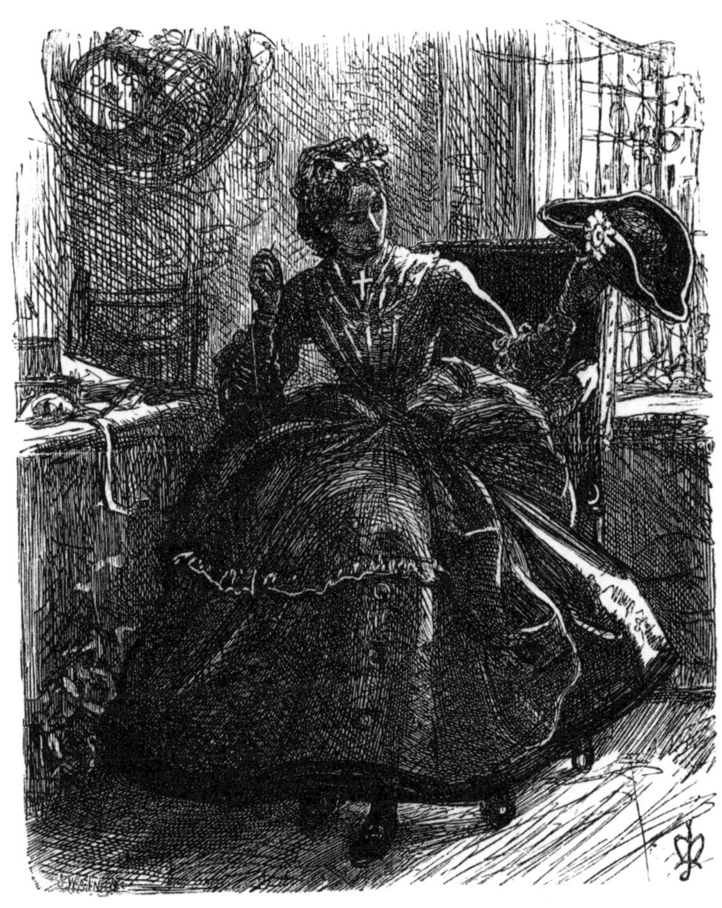

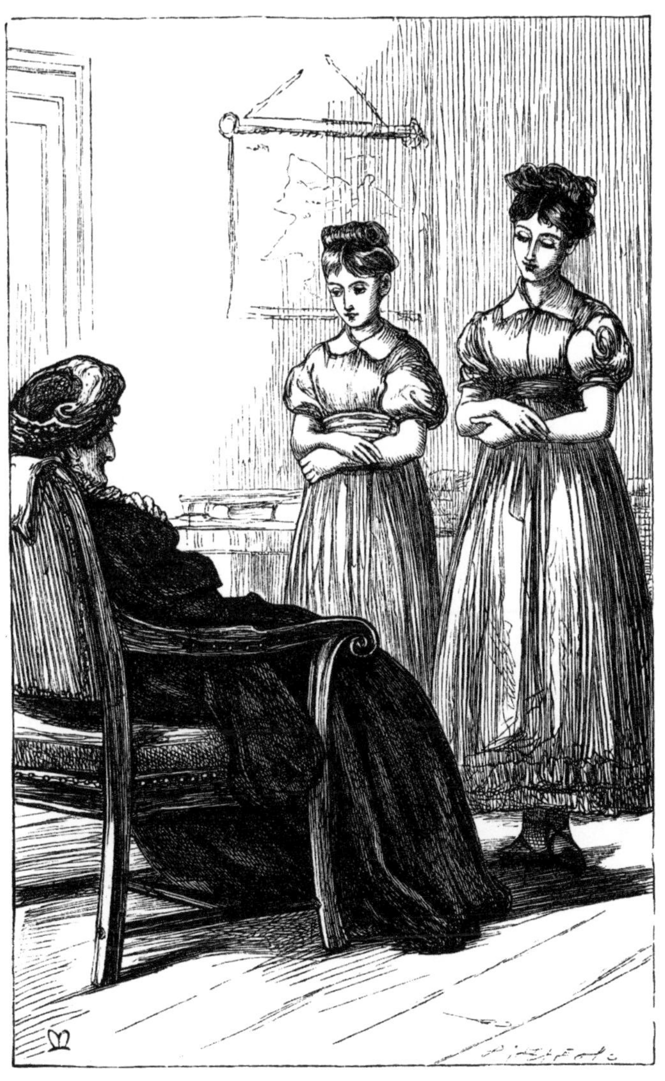

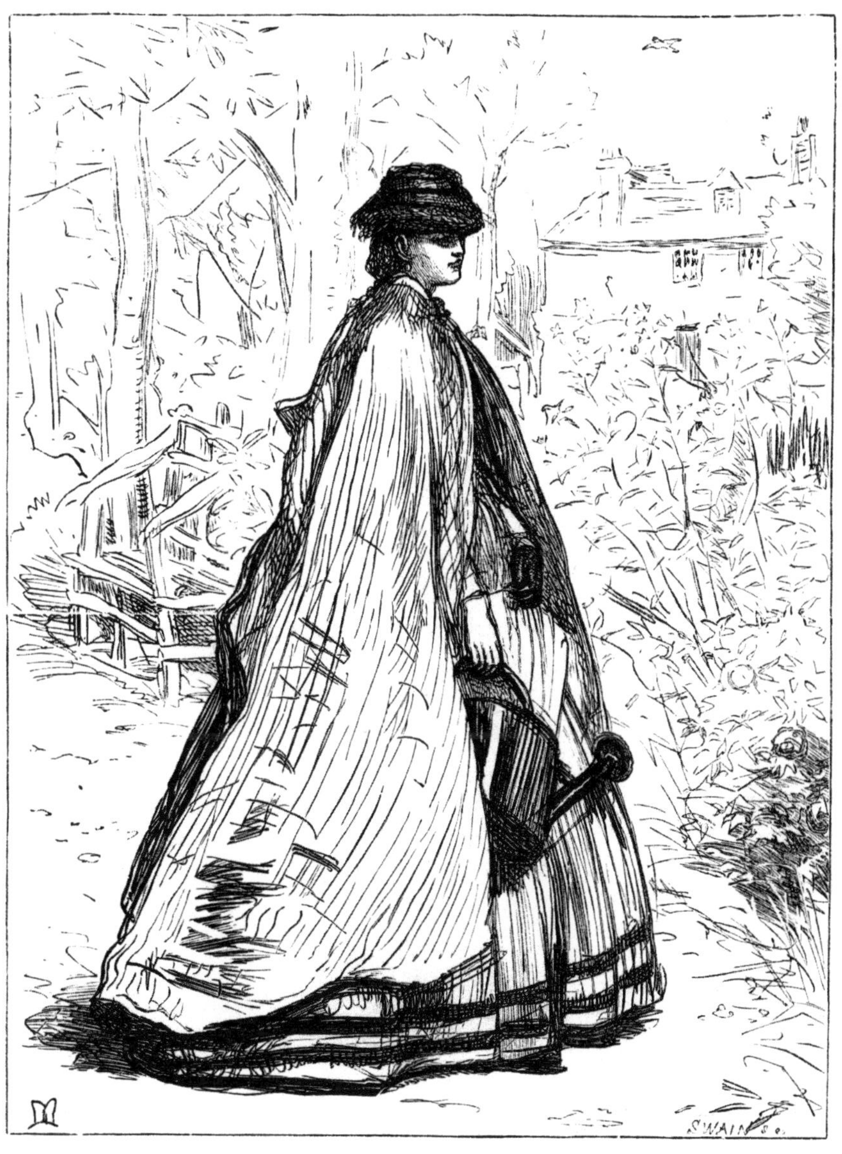
SWAIN

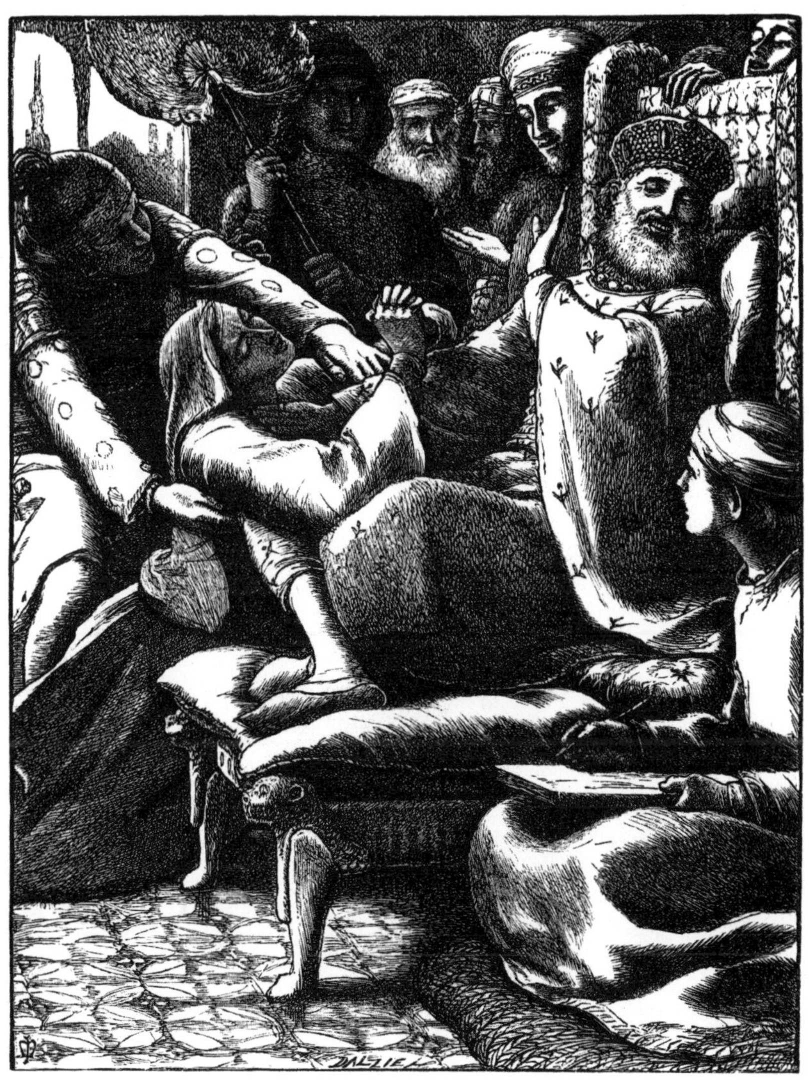
DALZIEL

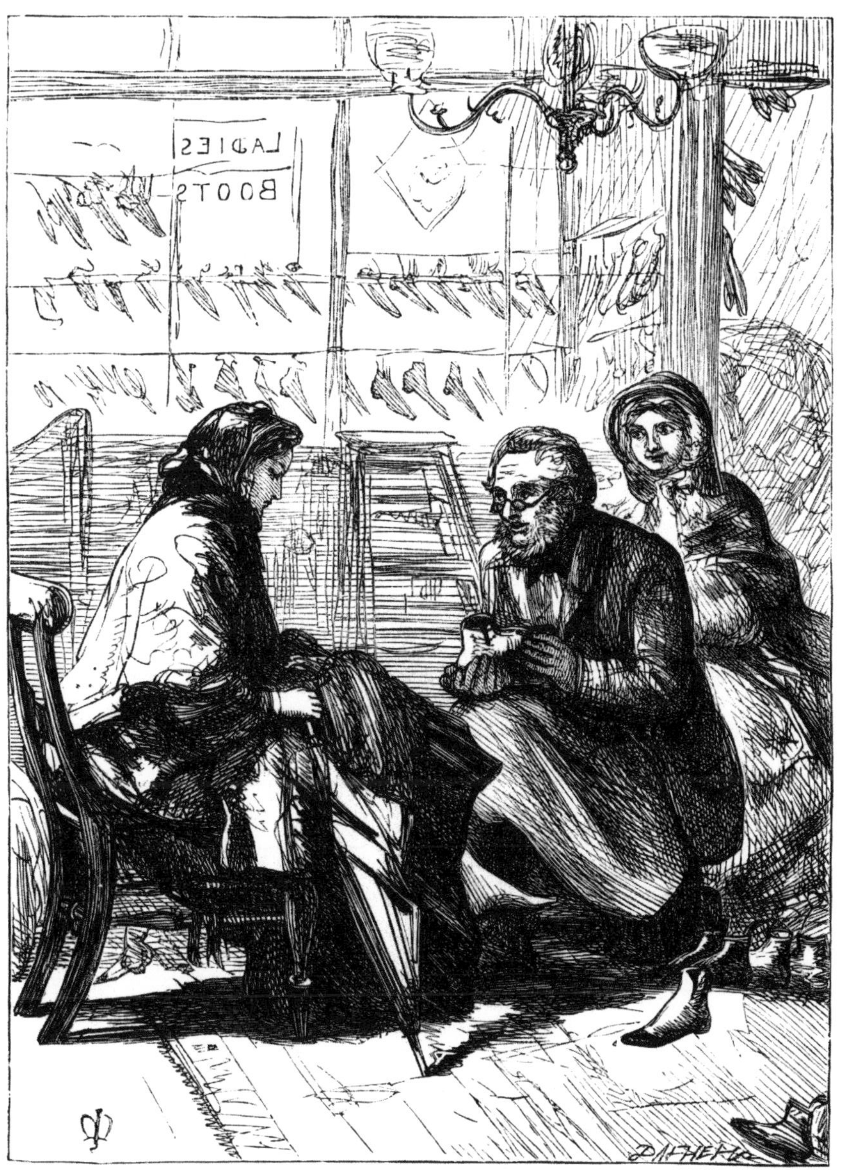
LADIES
BOOTS

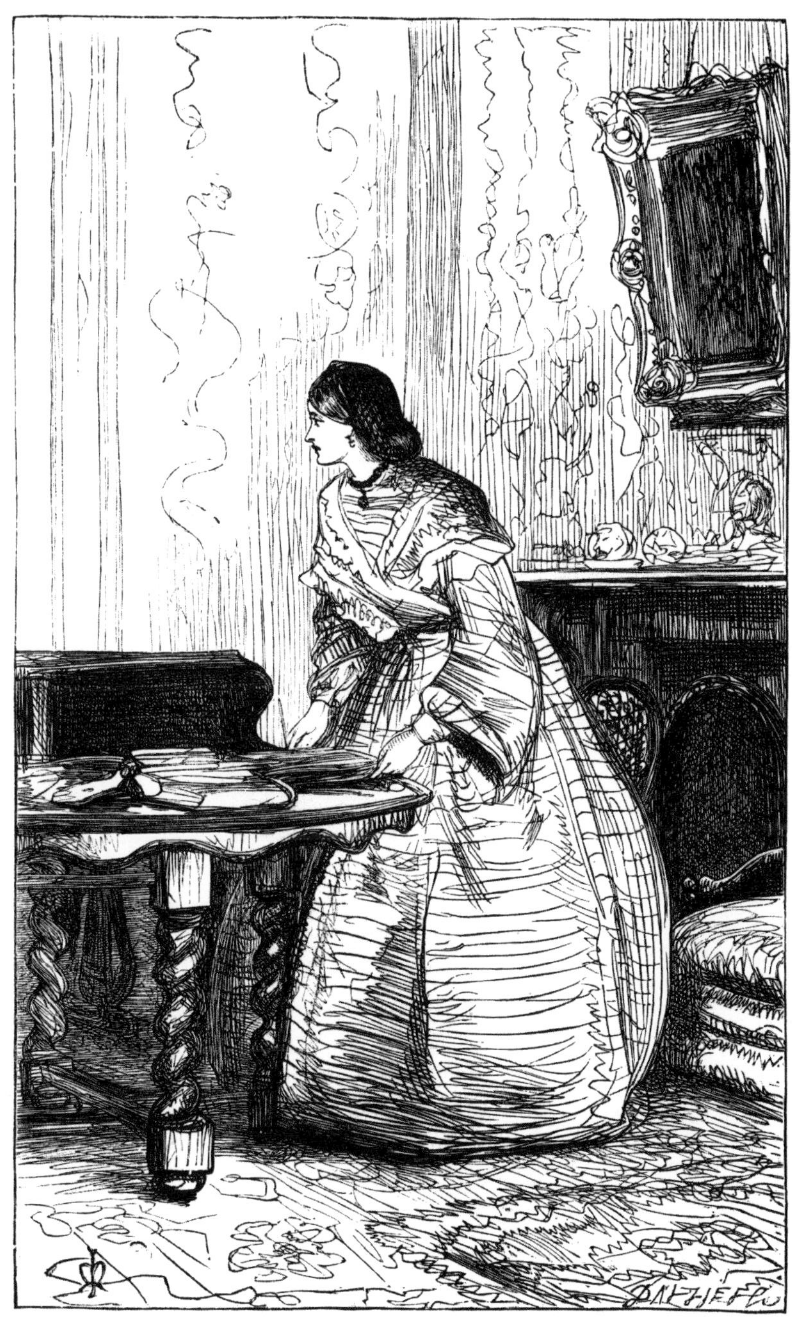

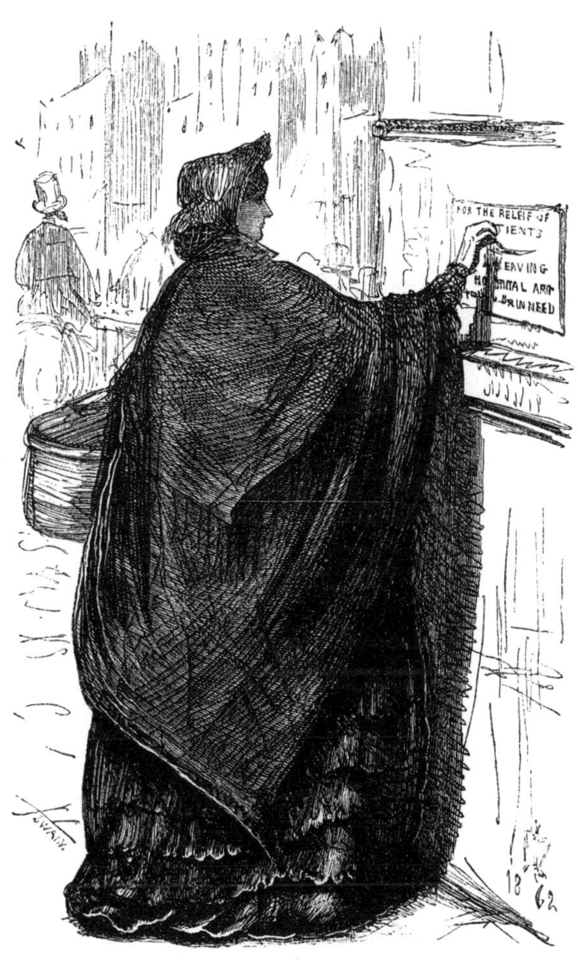
FOR THE RELEIF OF
TIENTS
EAVING
IN NEED
1862

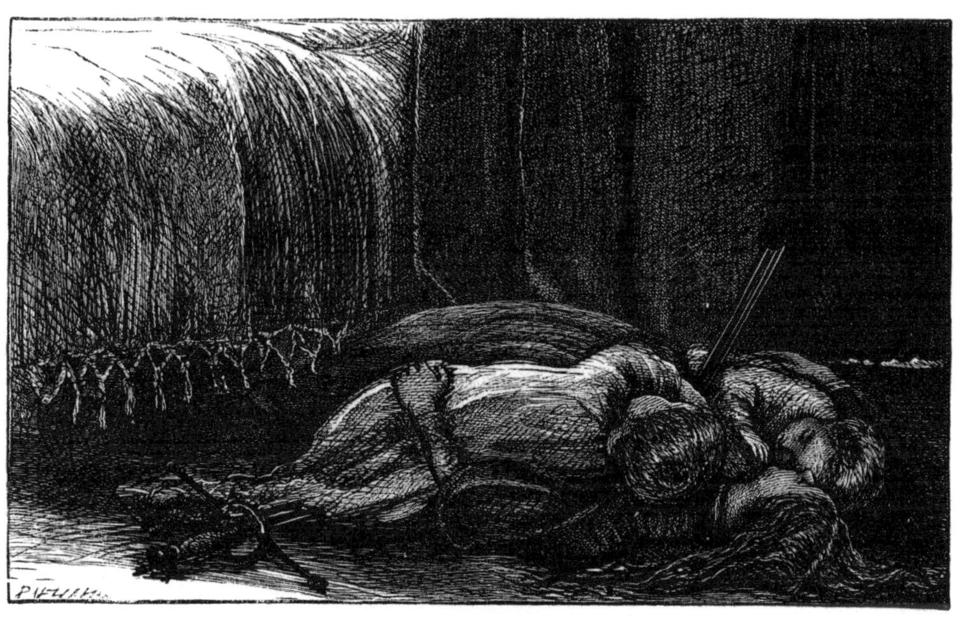

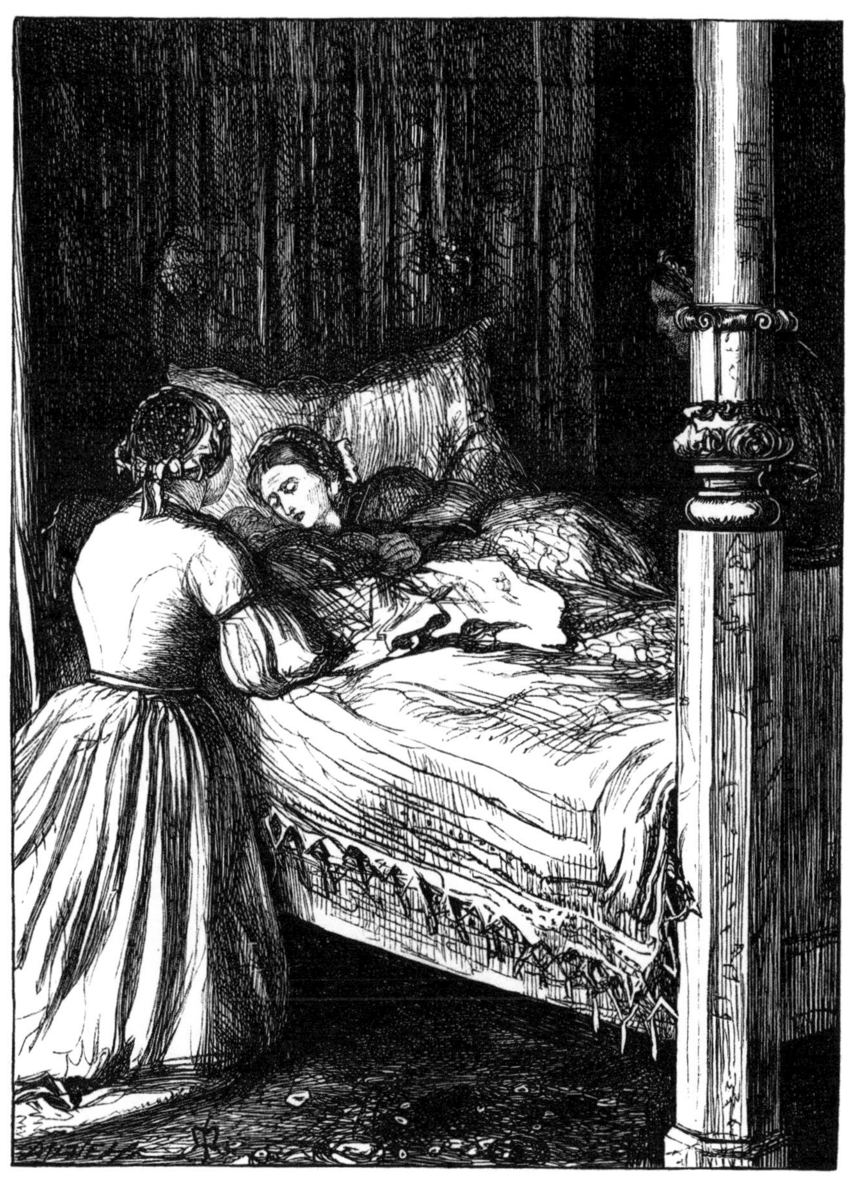

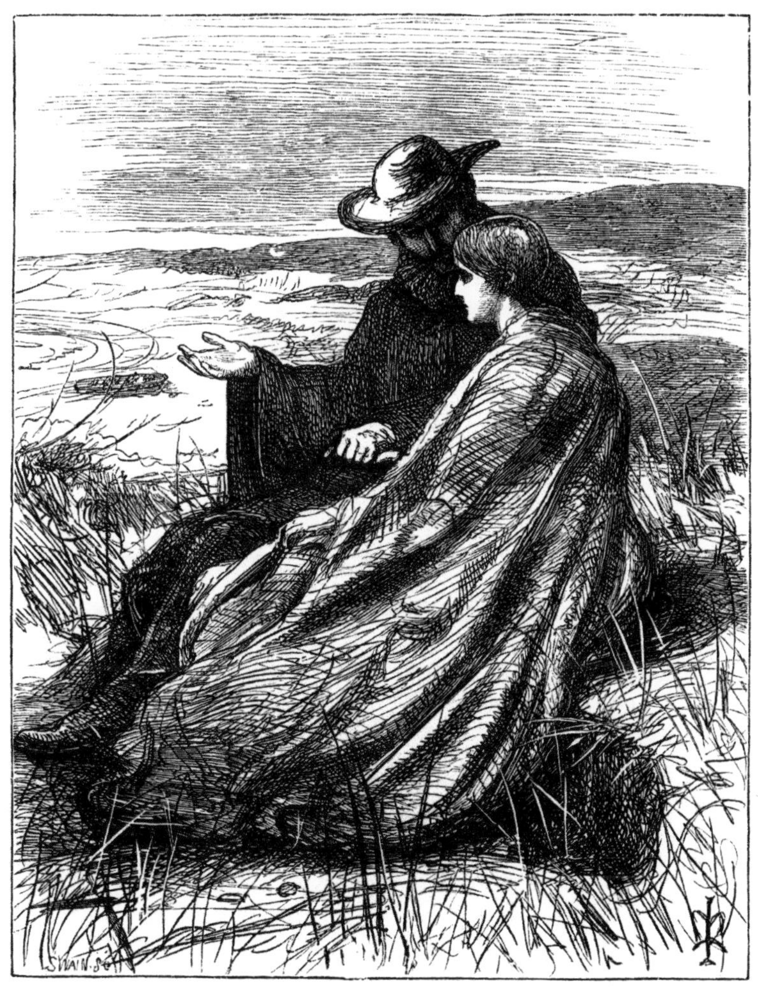

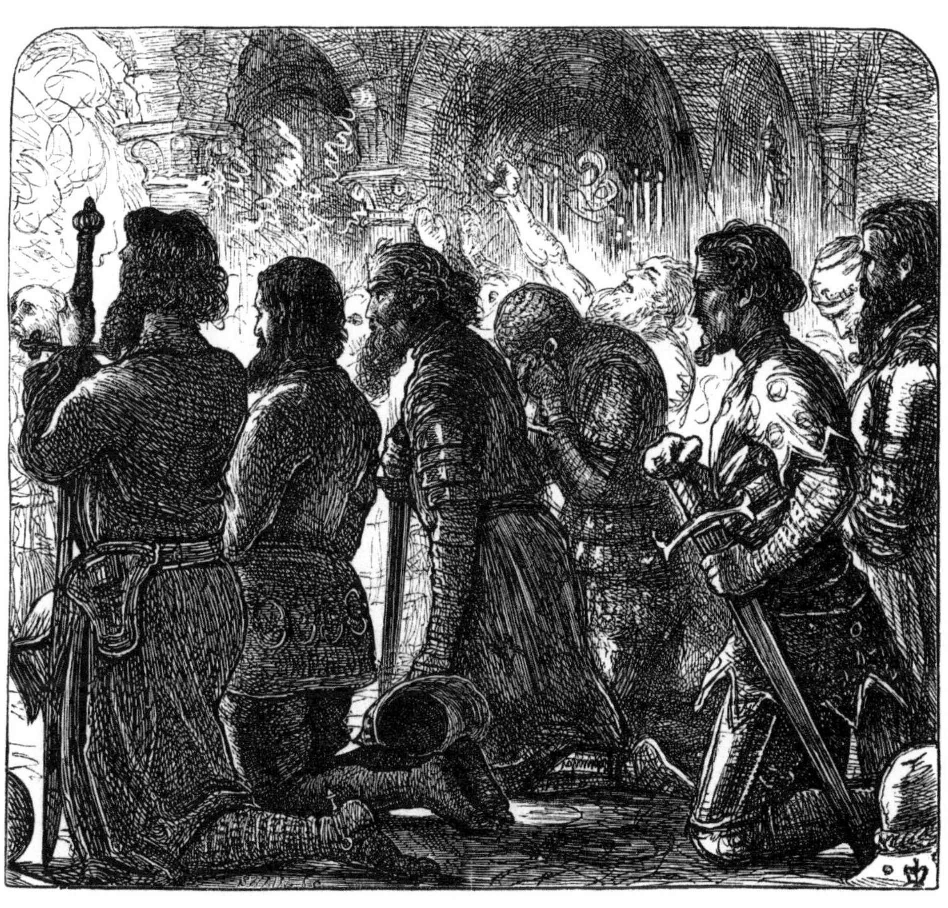

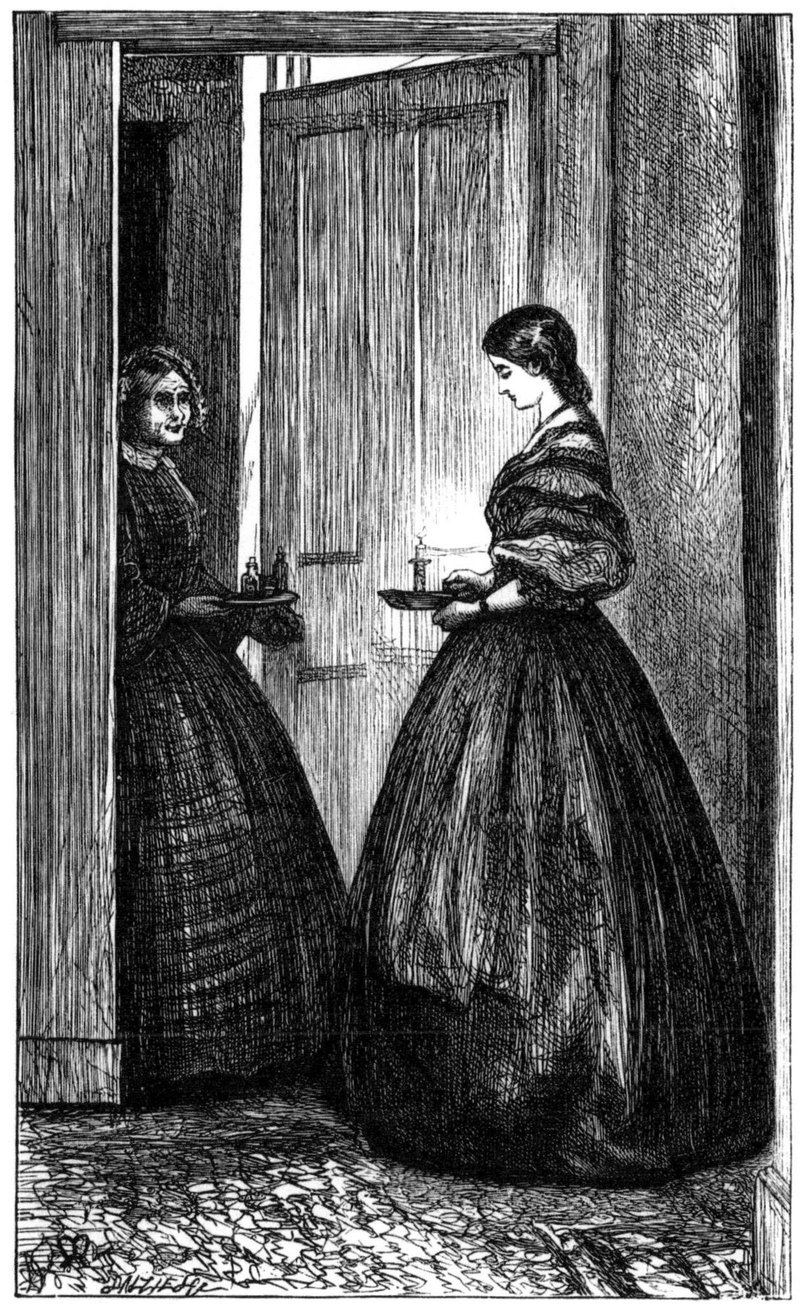

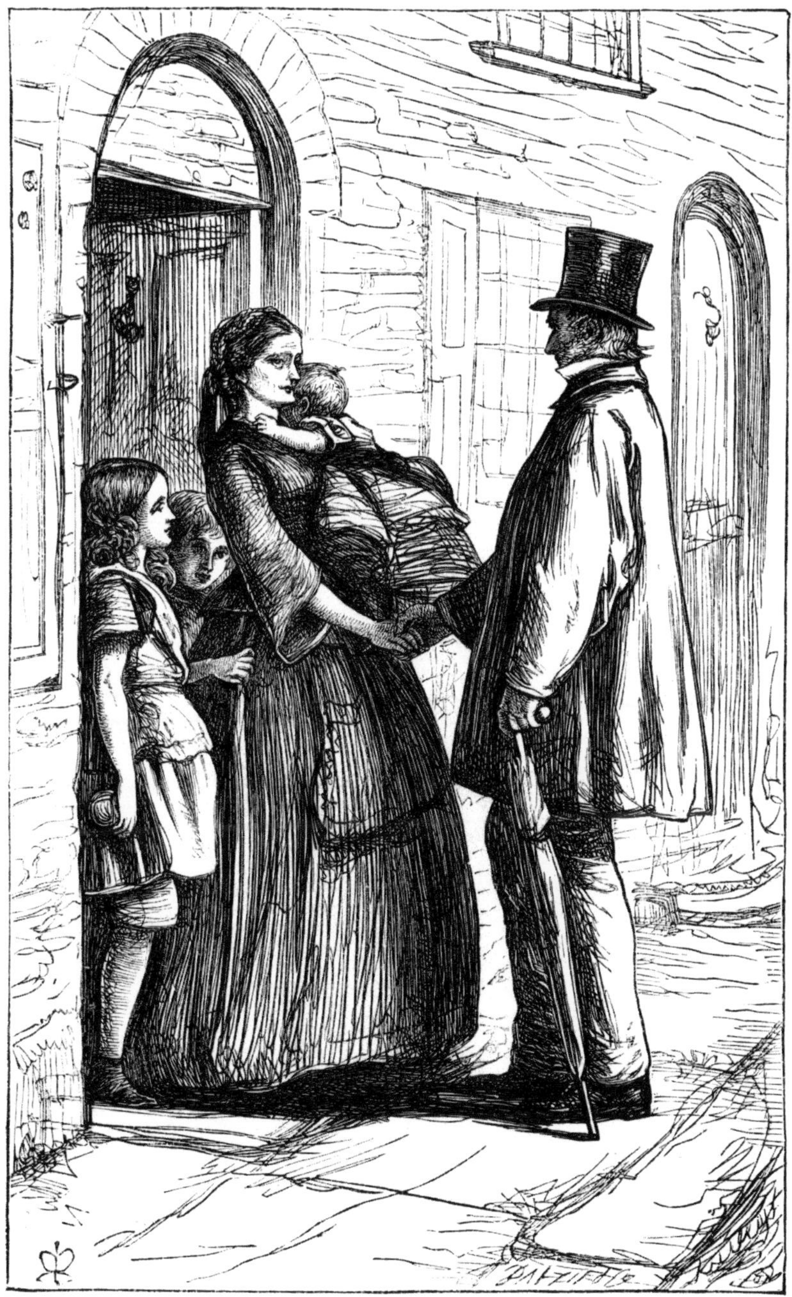

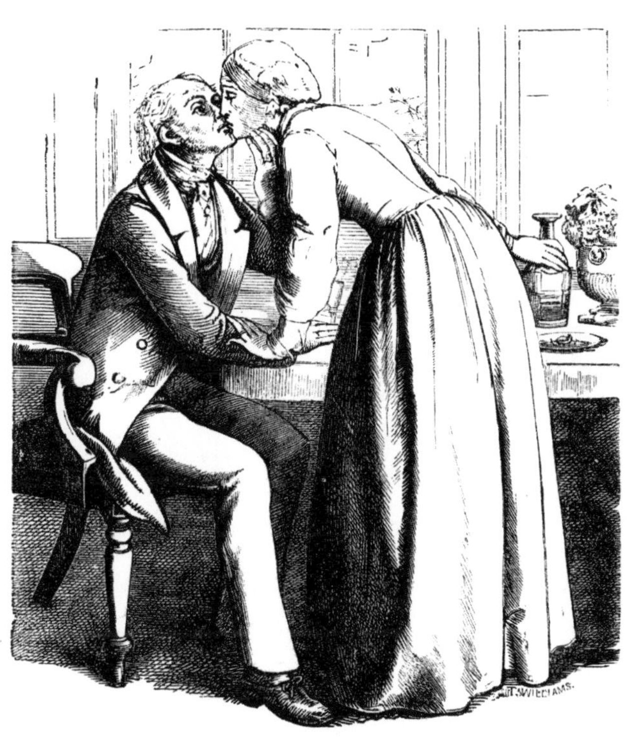

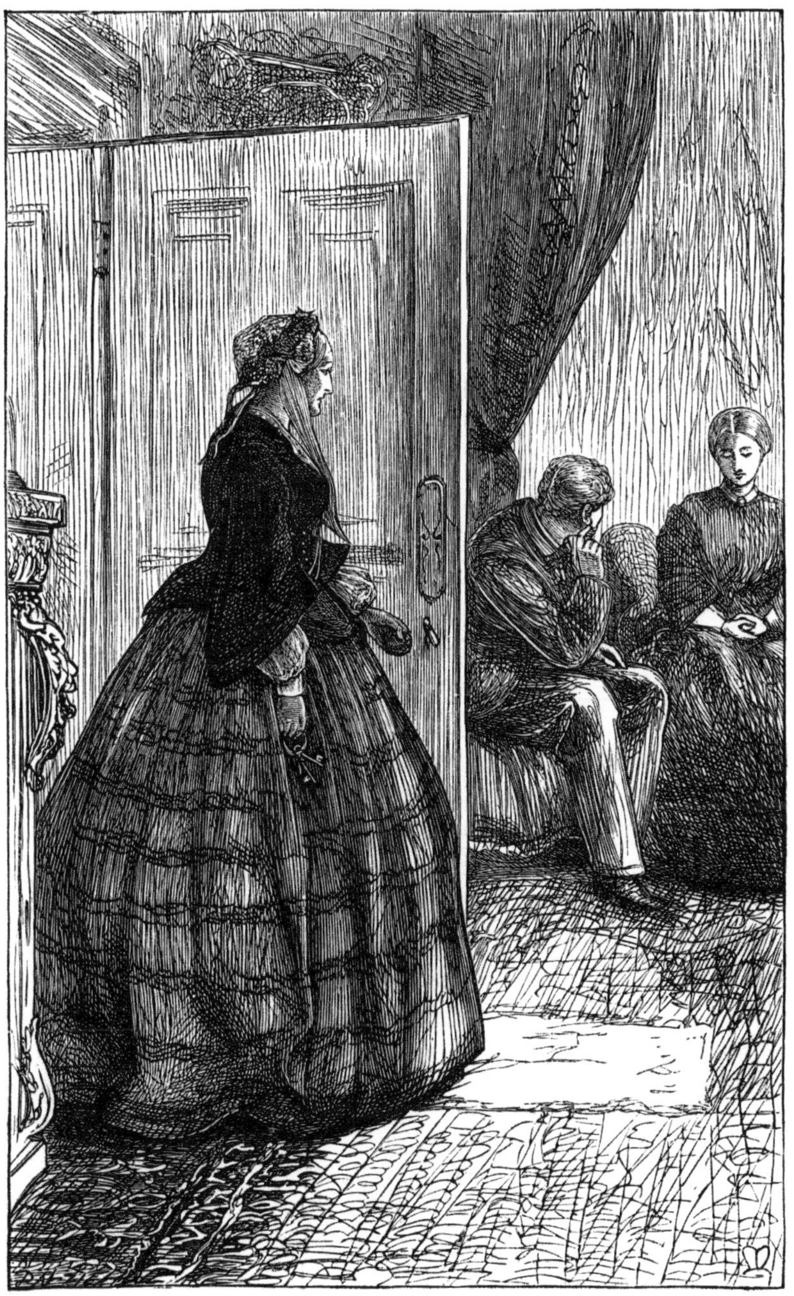

49

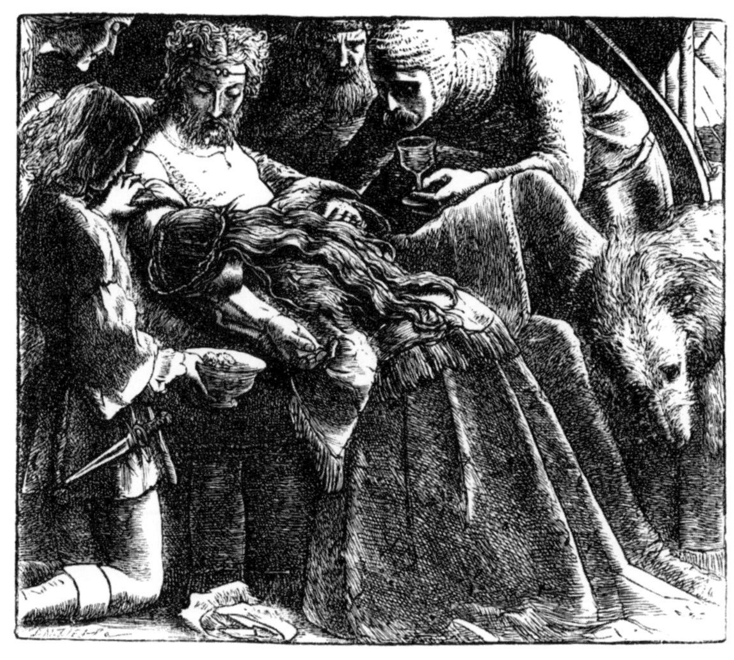

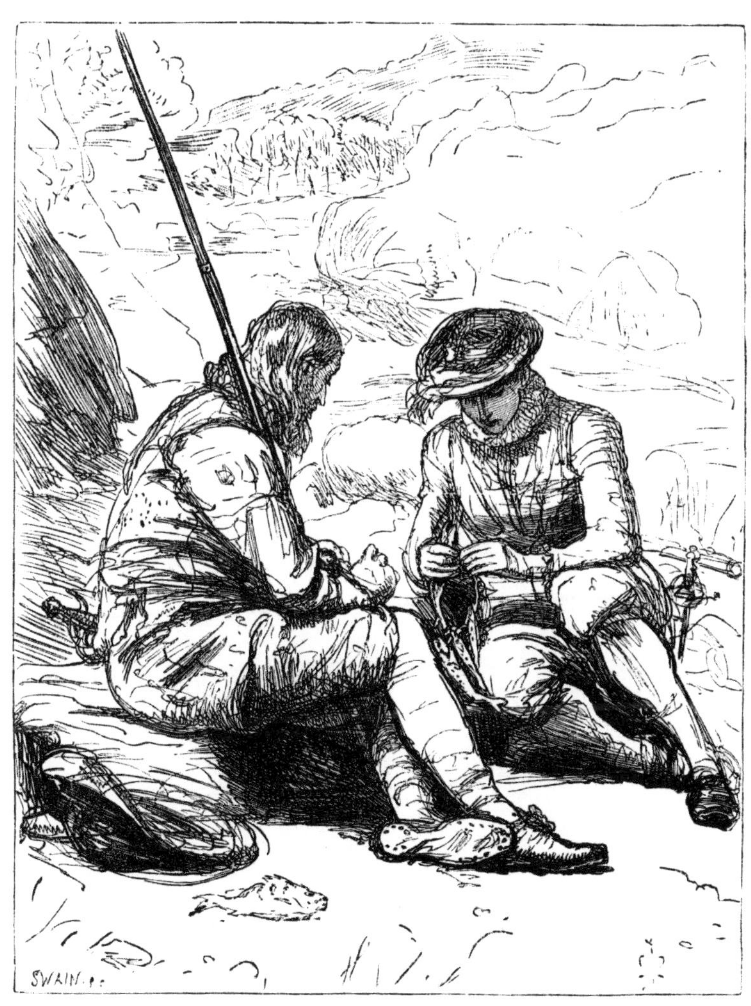
SWAIN

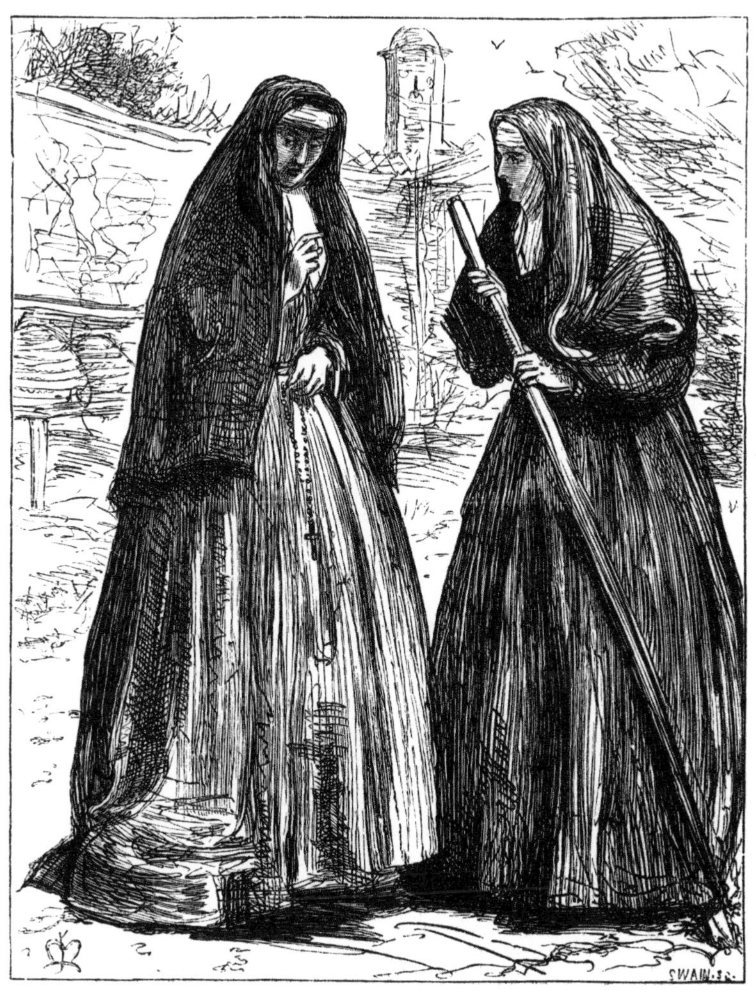
SWAIN. sc.

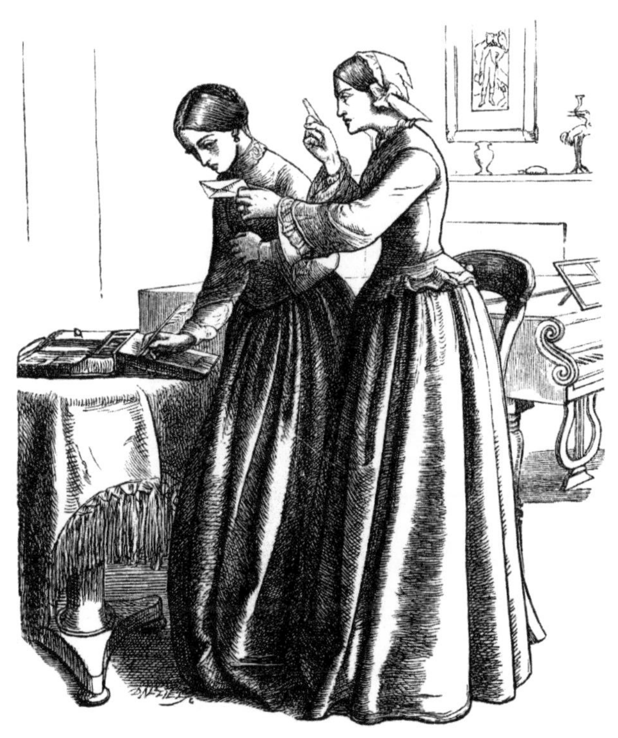

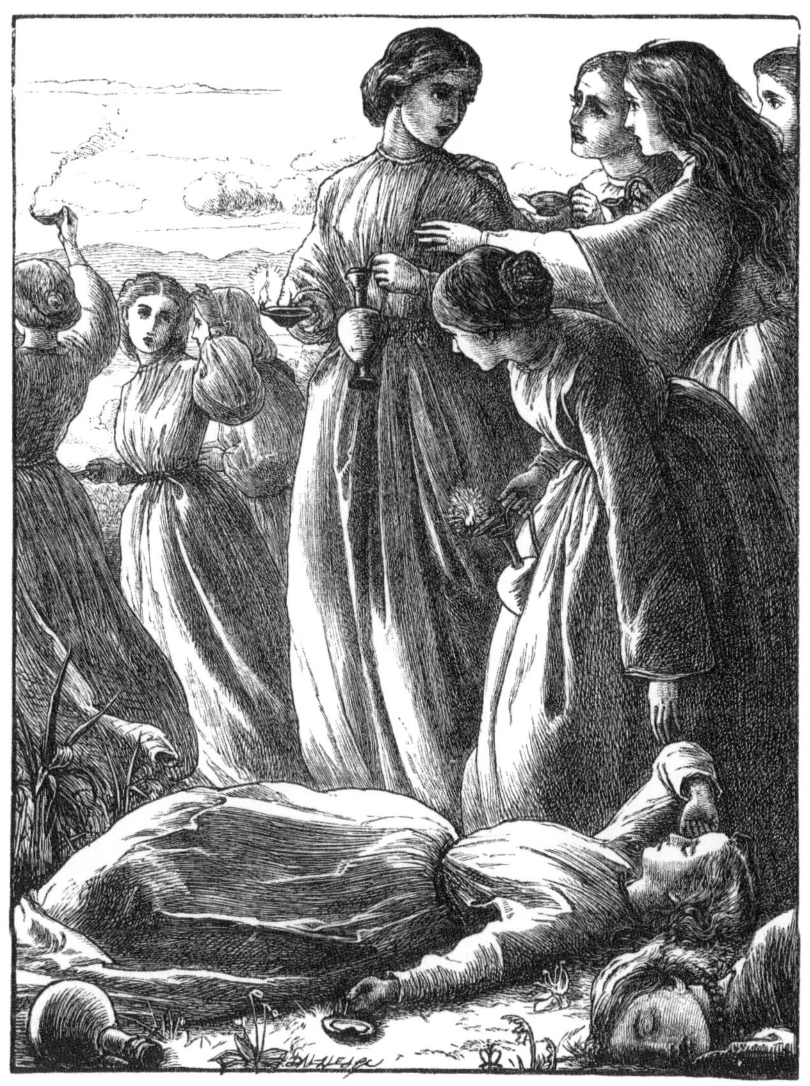

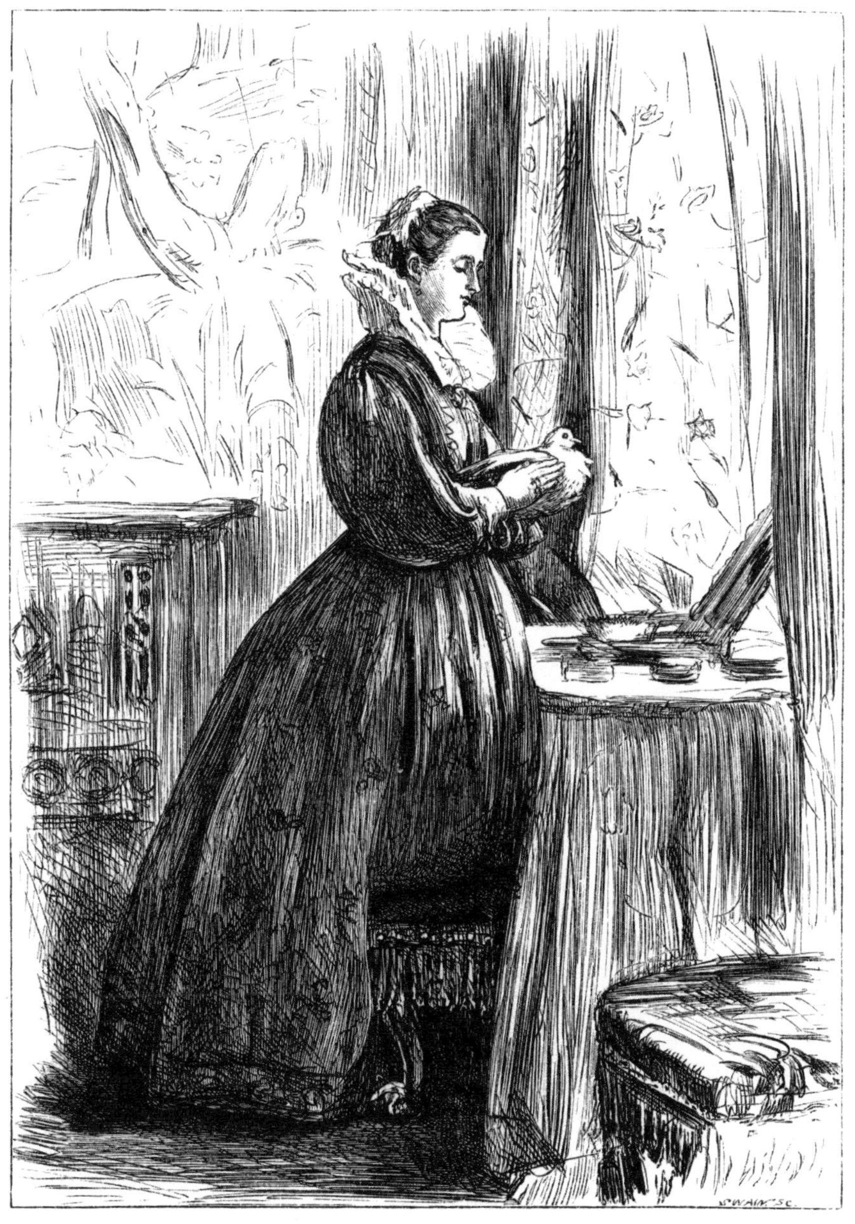
SWAIN SC.

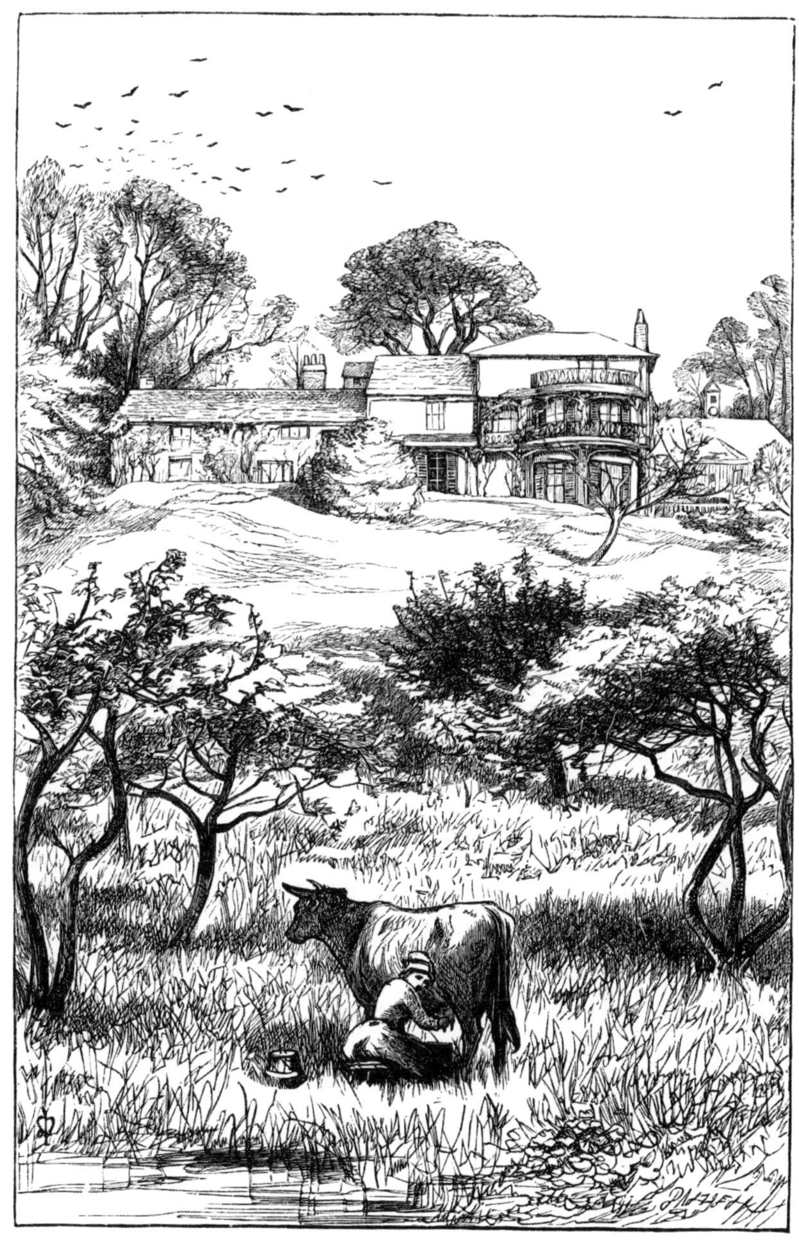

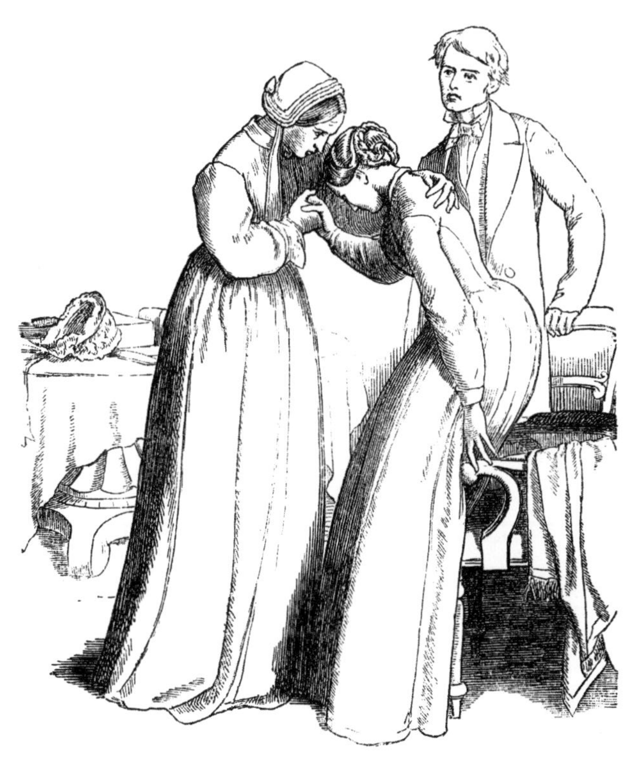

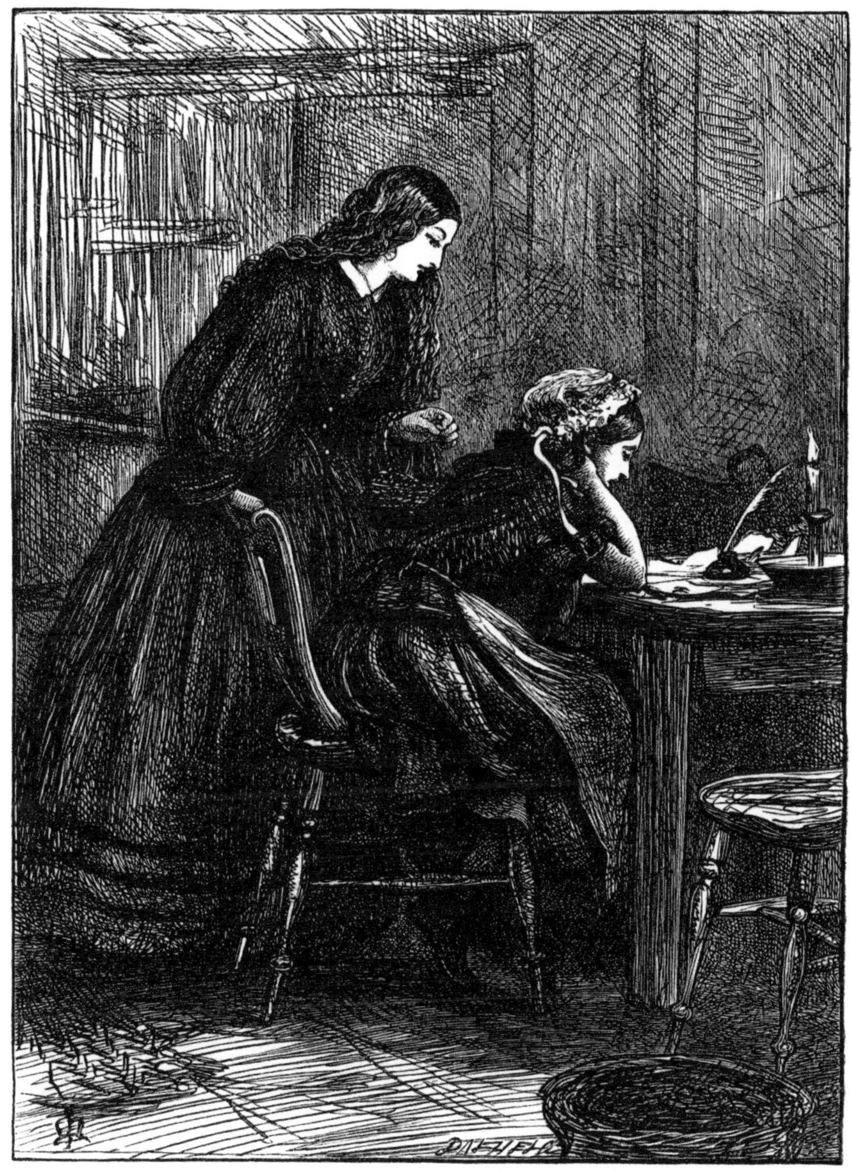

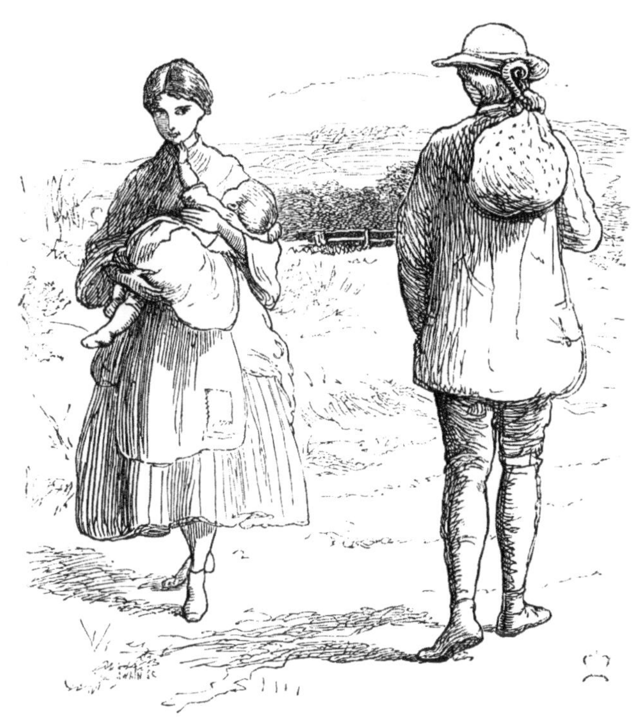

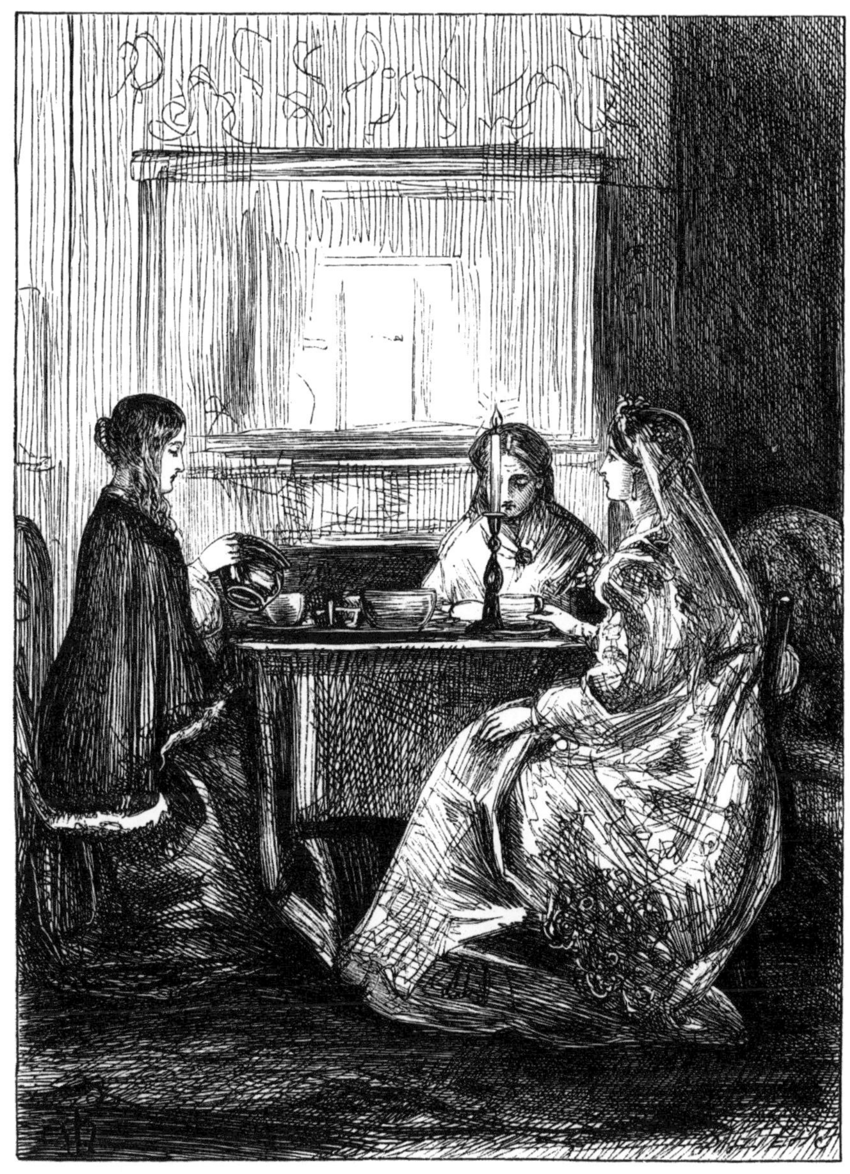

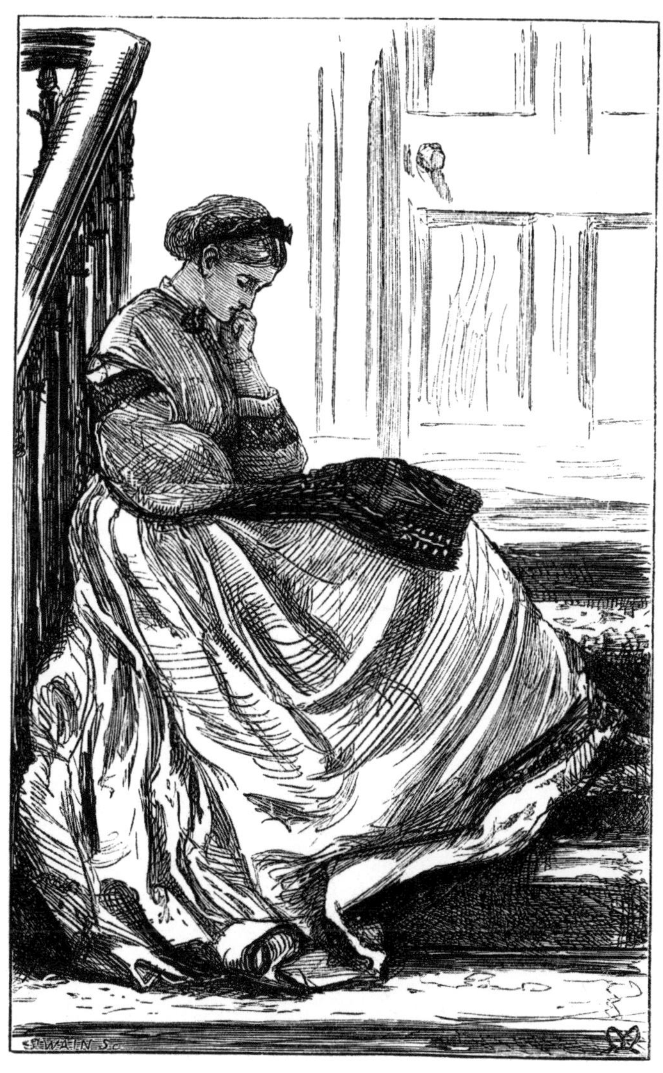

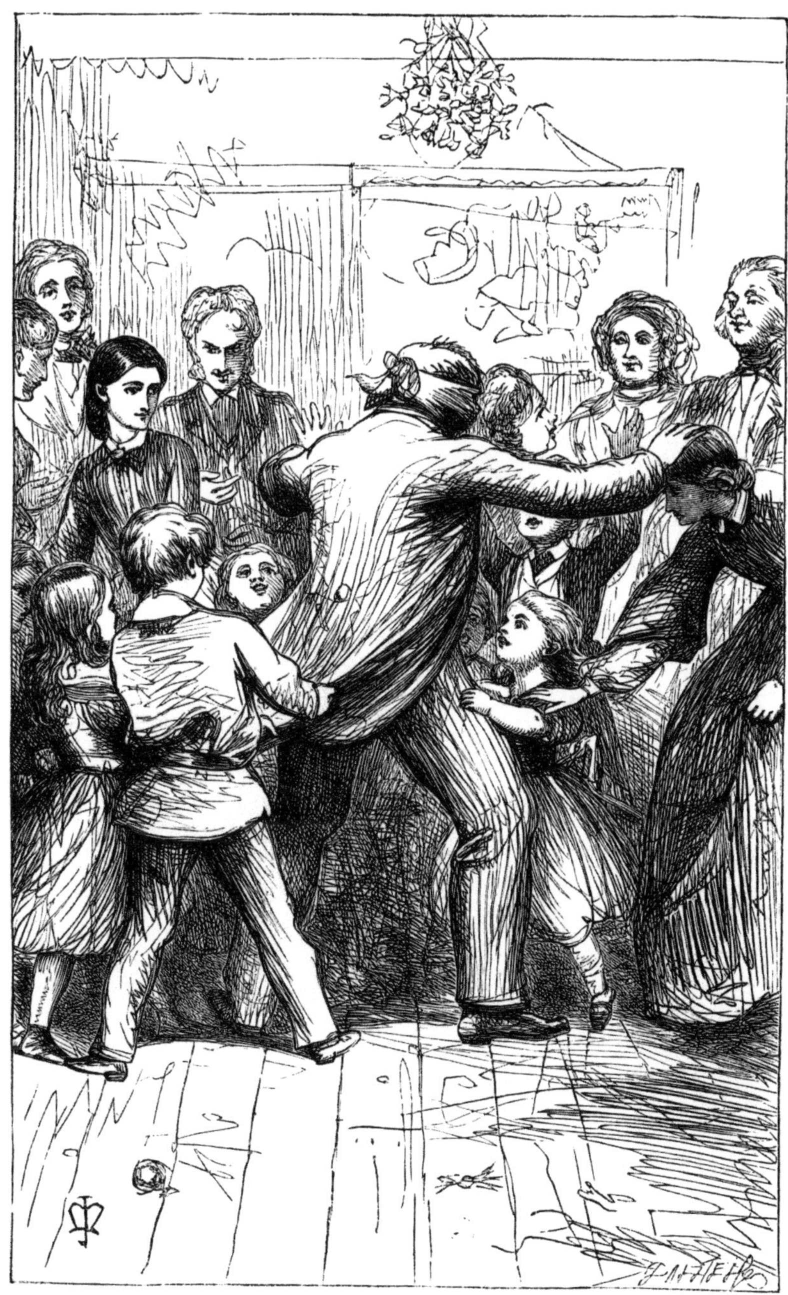

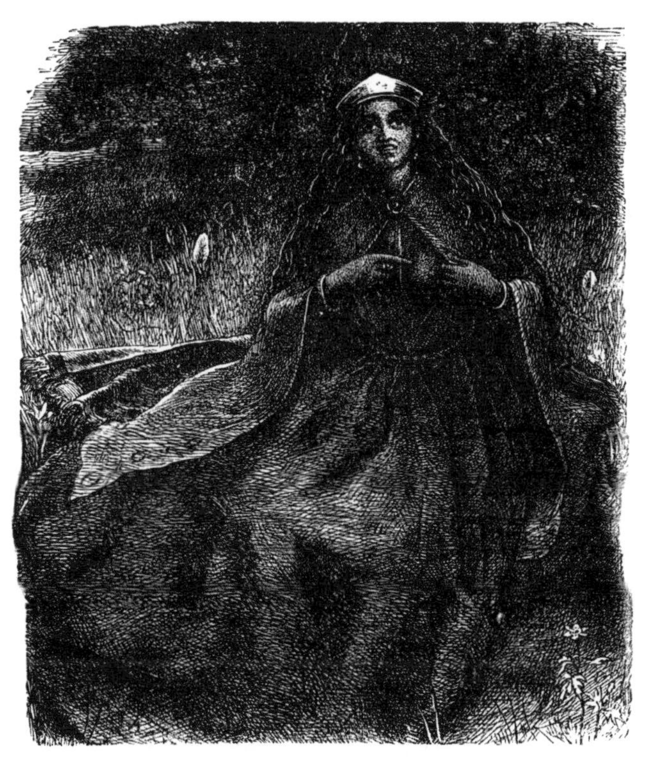

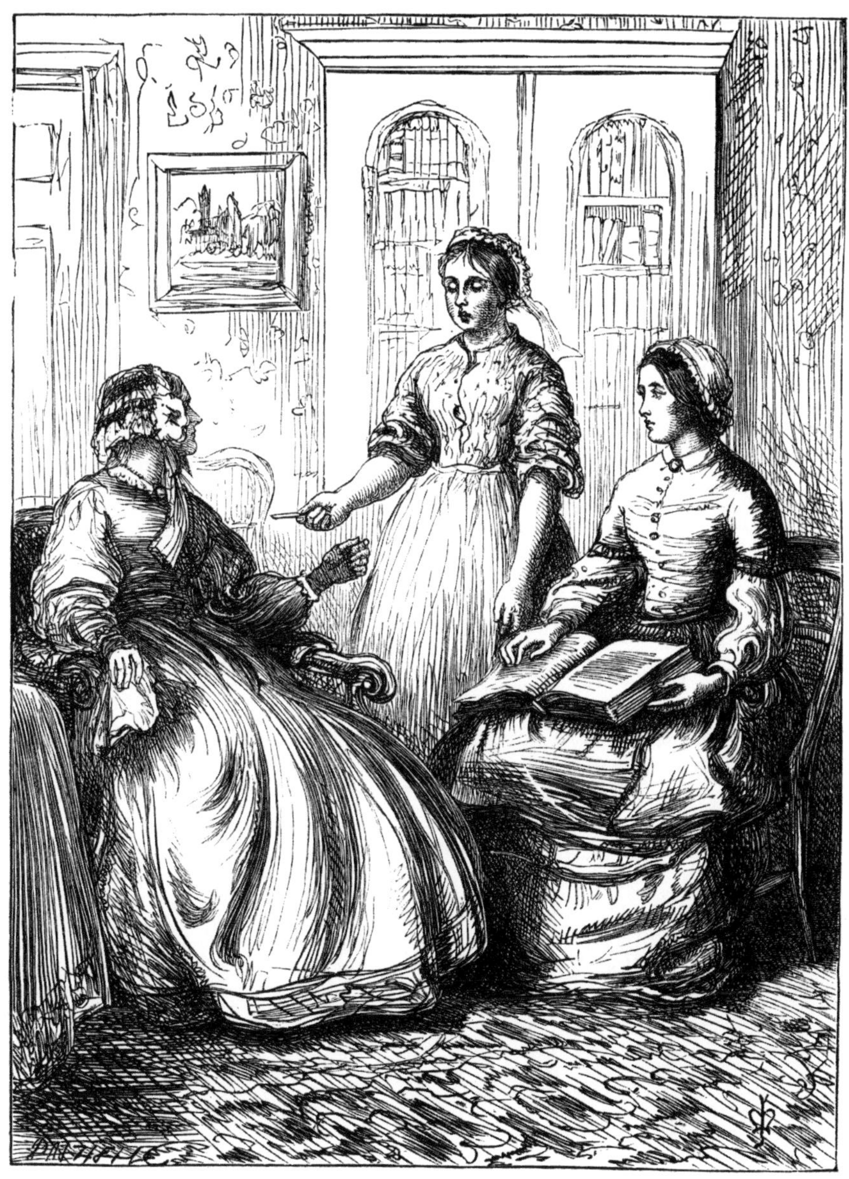

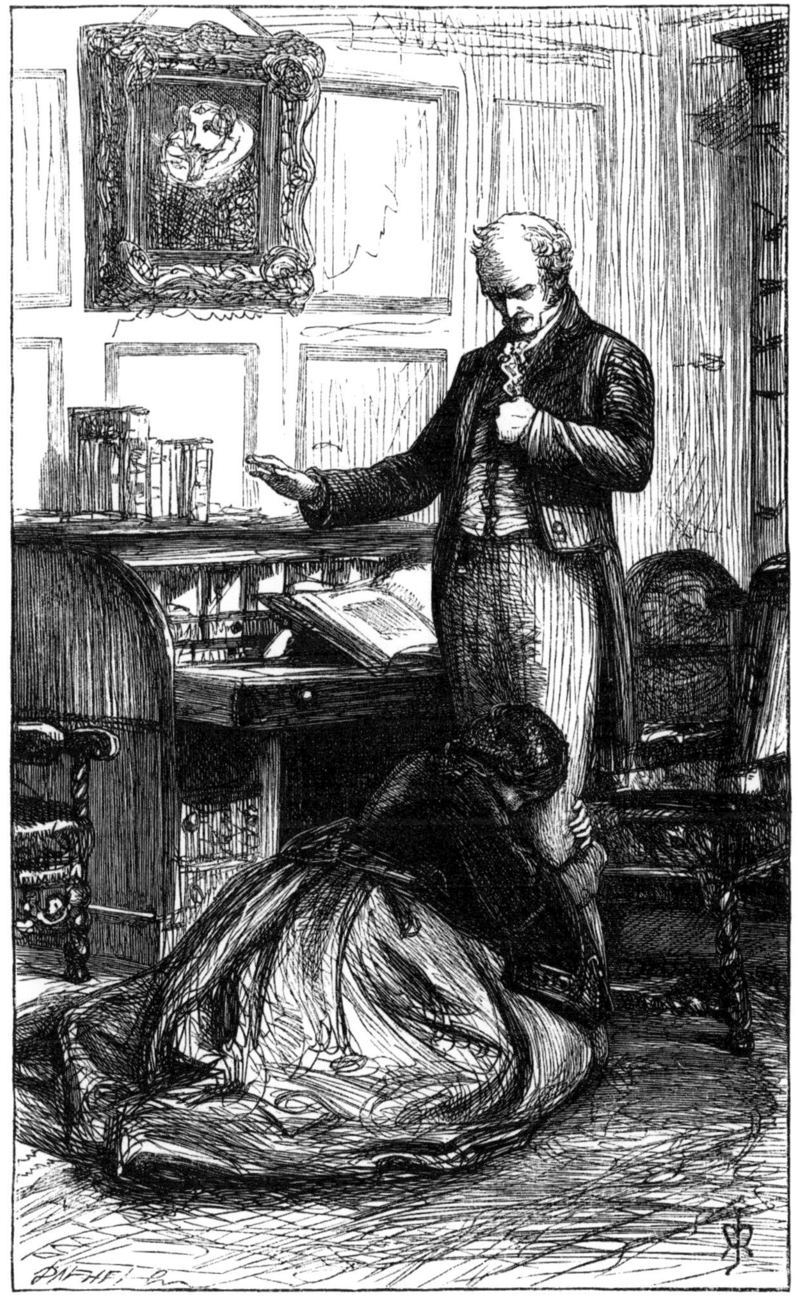

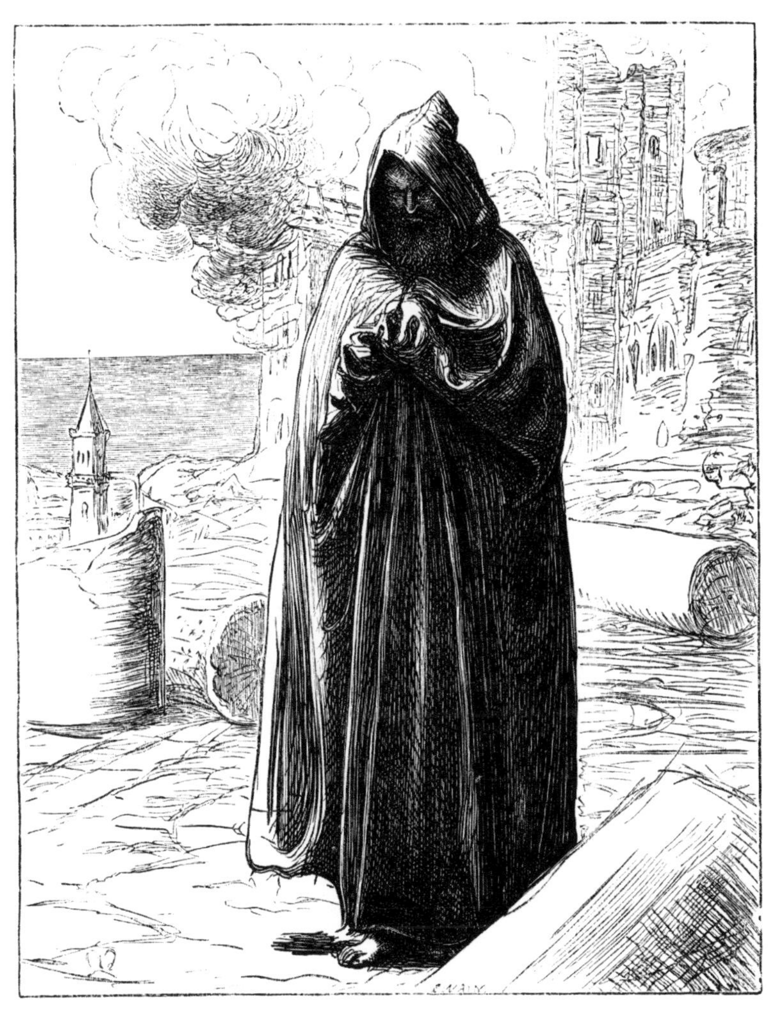

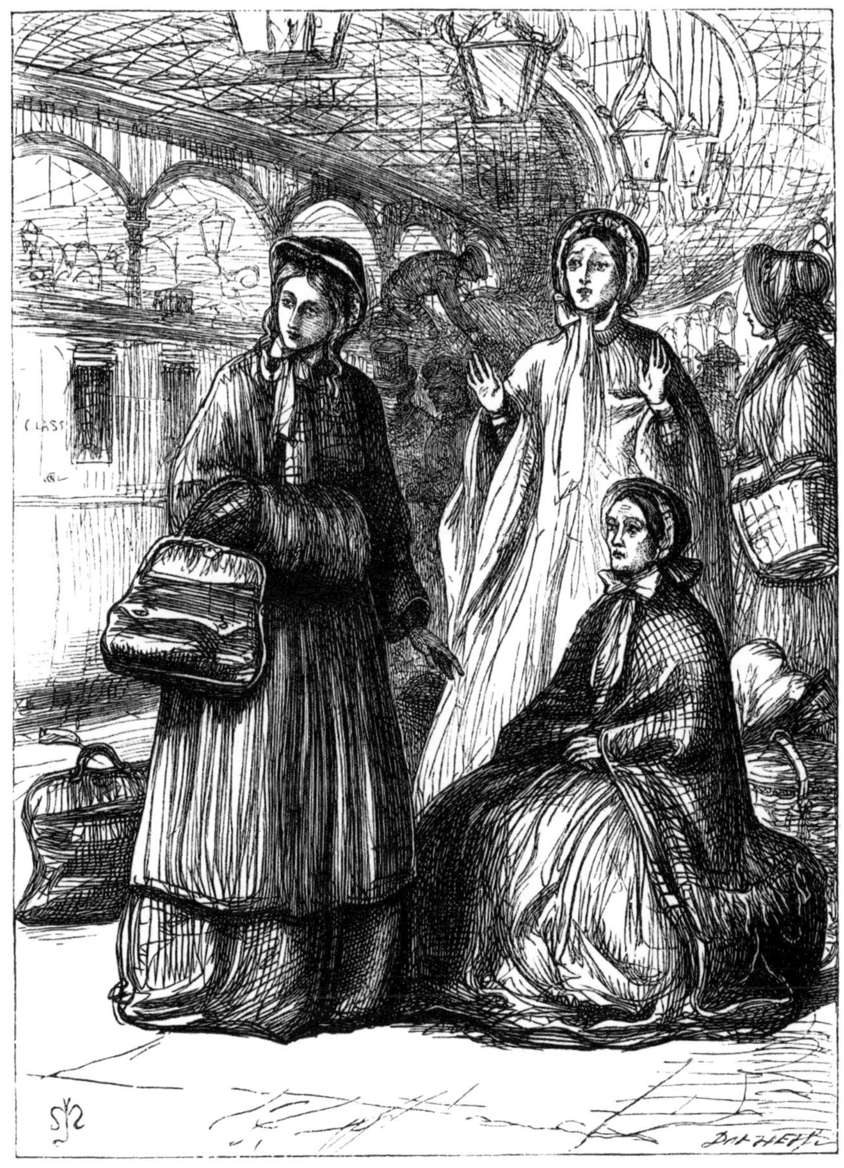
CLASS

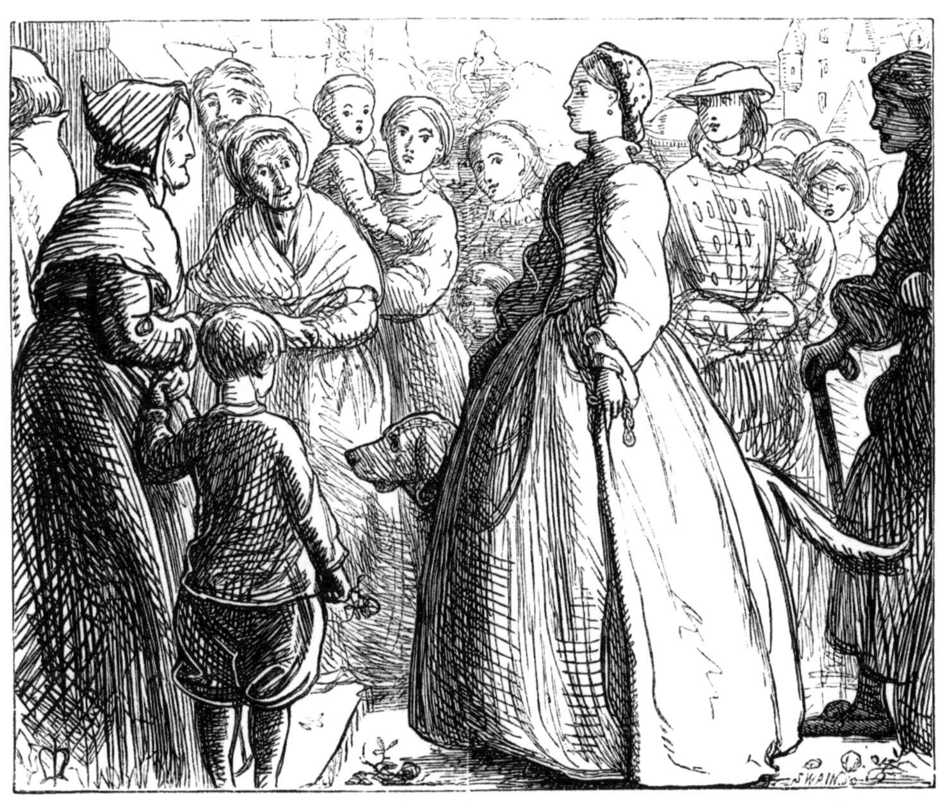
SWAIN

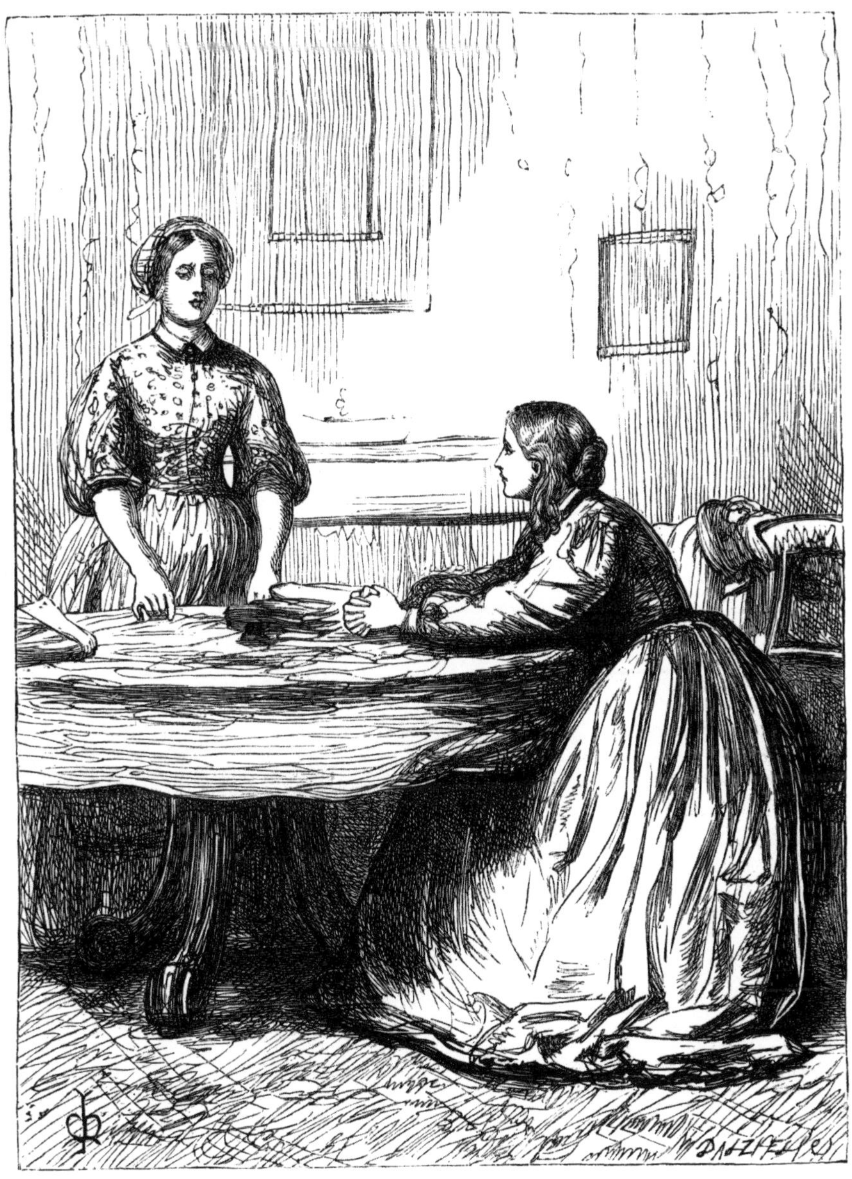

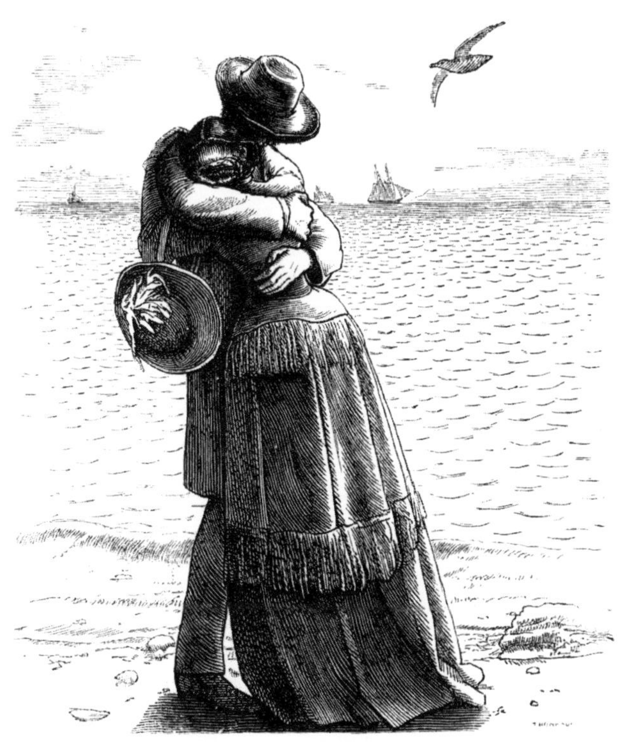

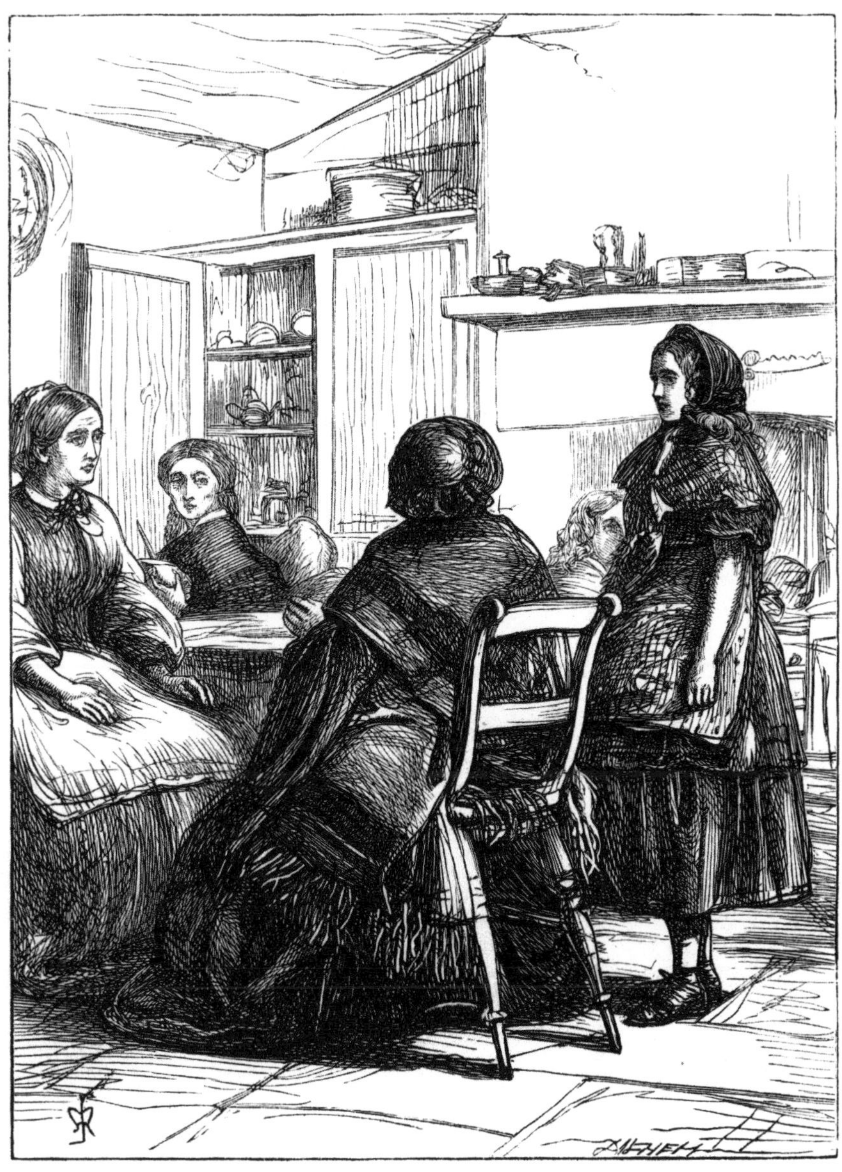

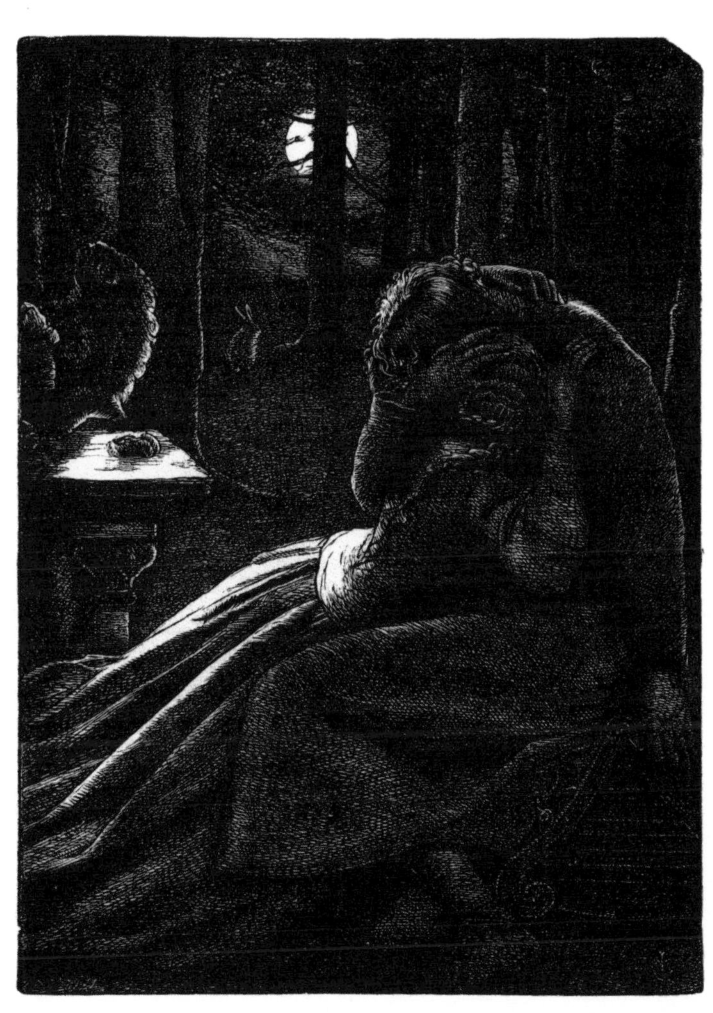

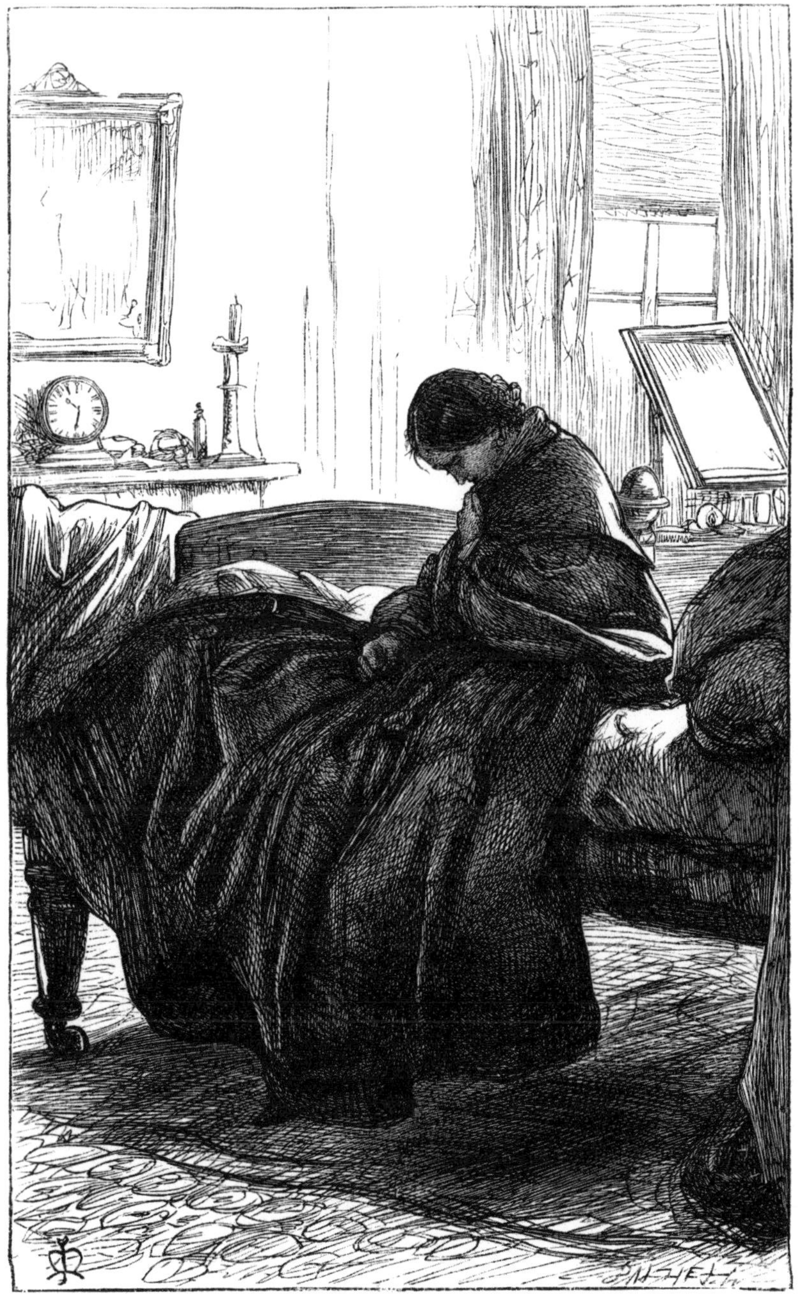

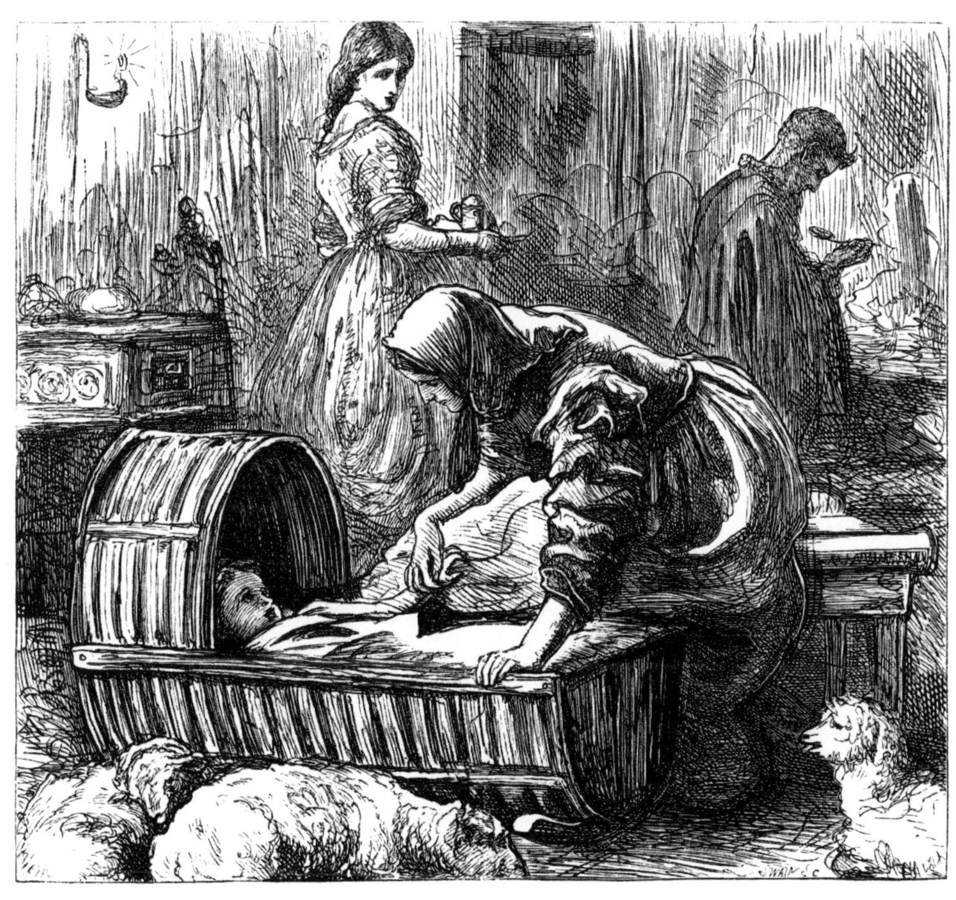

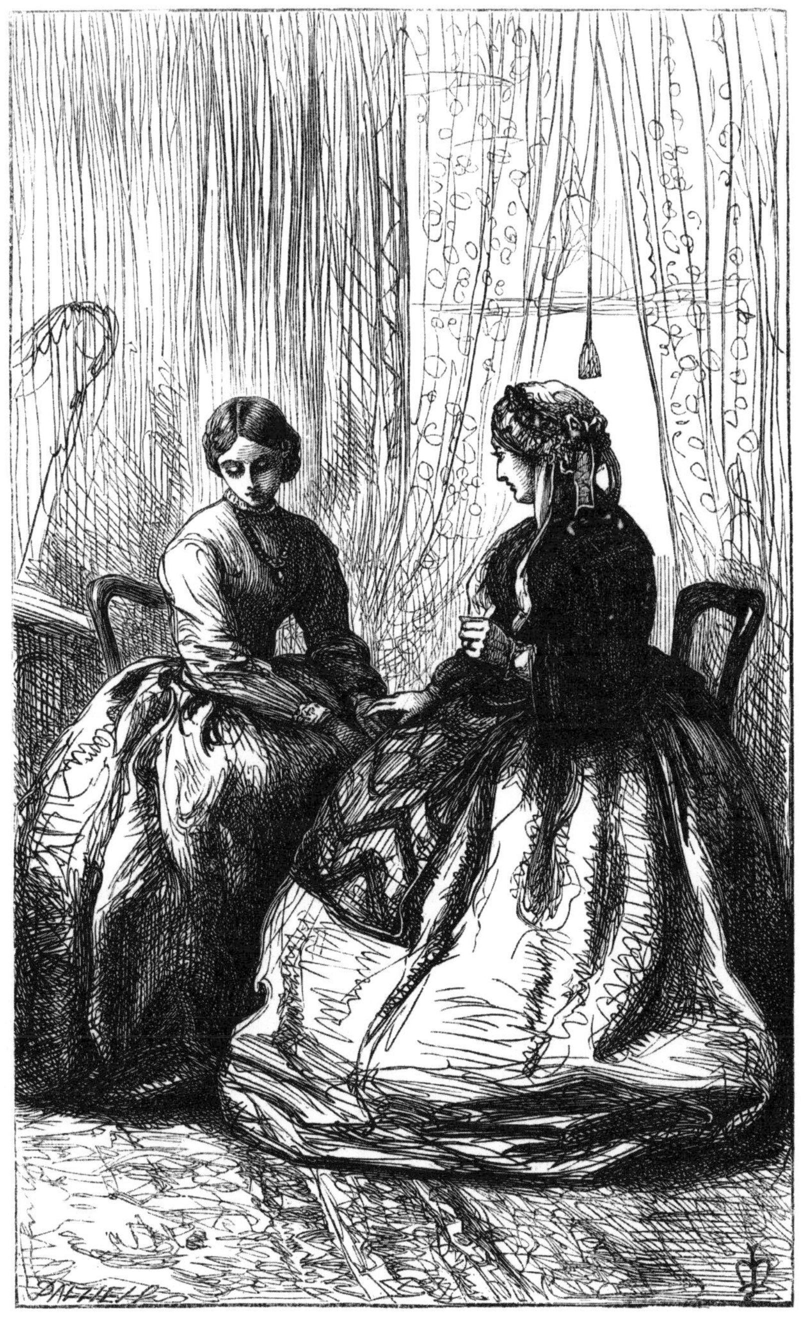

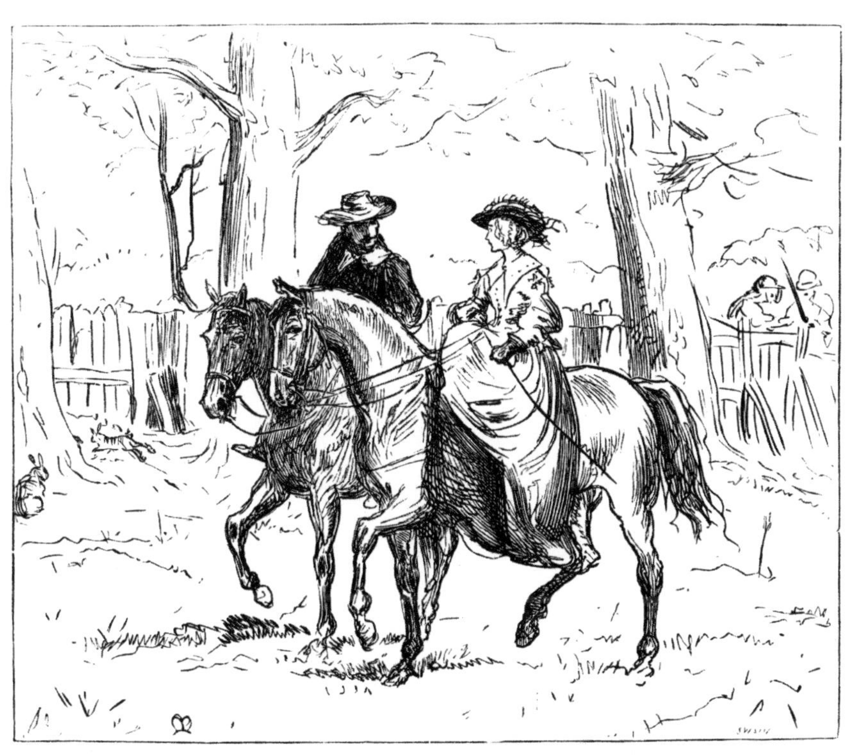

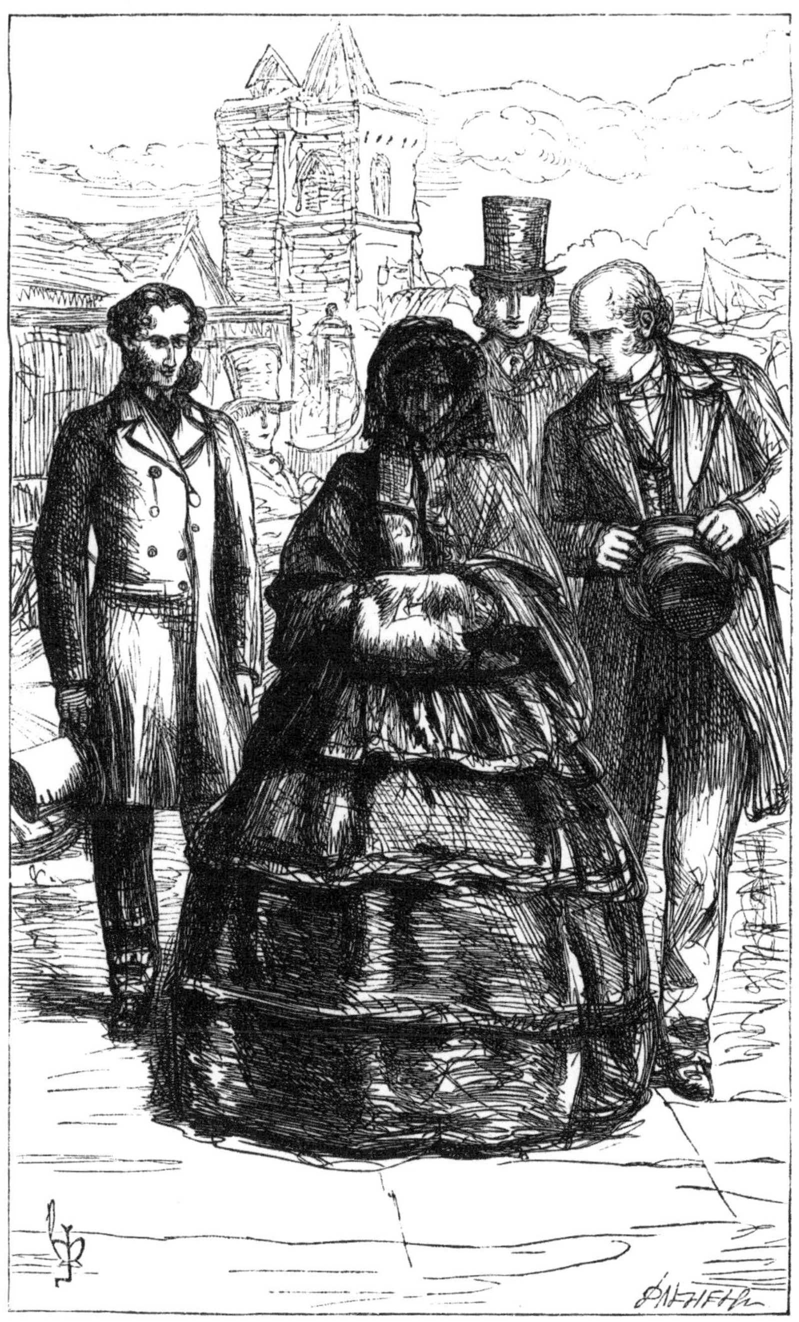

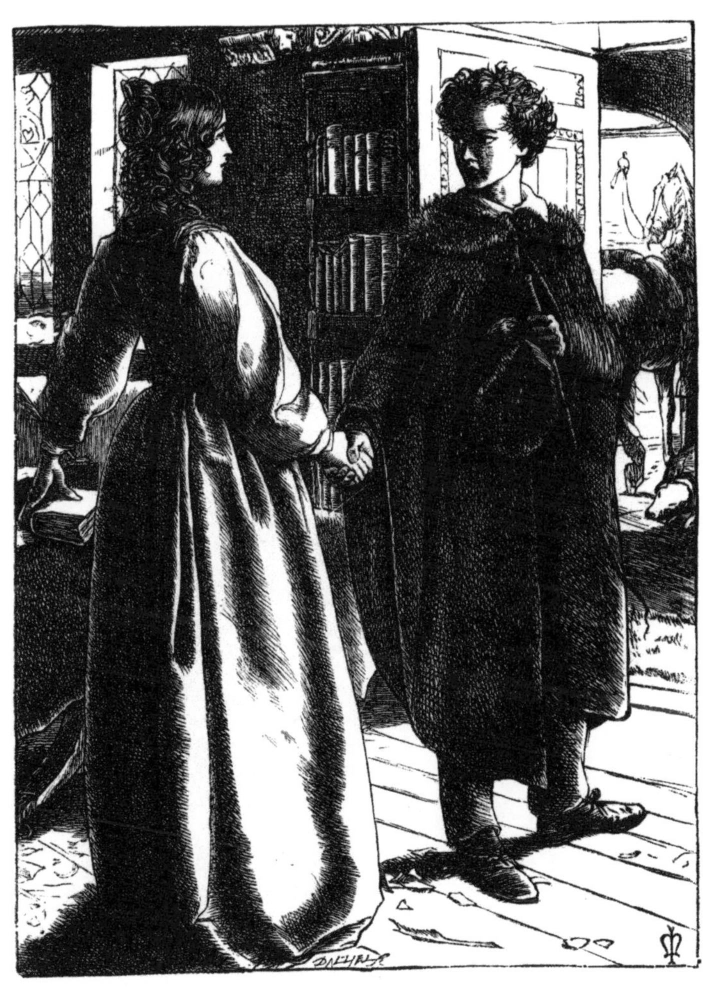

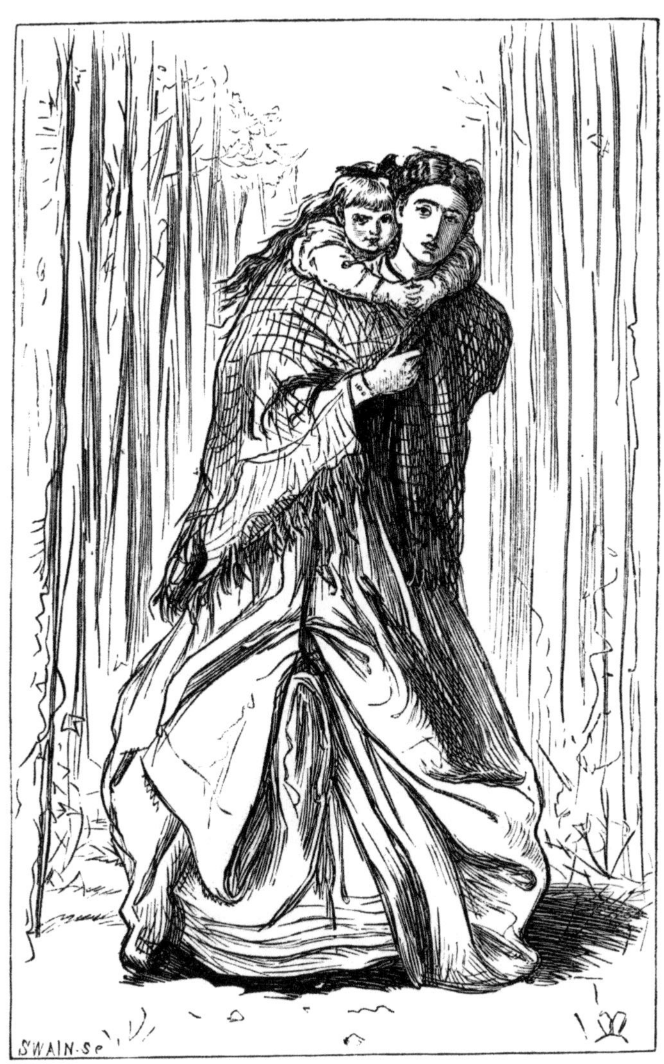
SWAIN·Sc

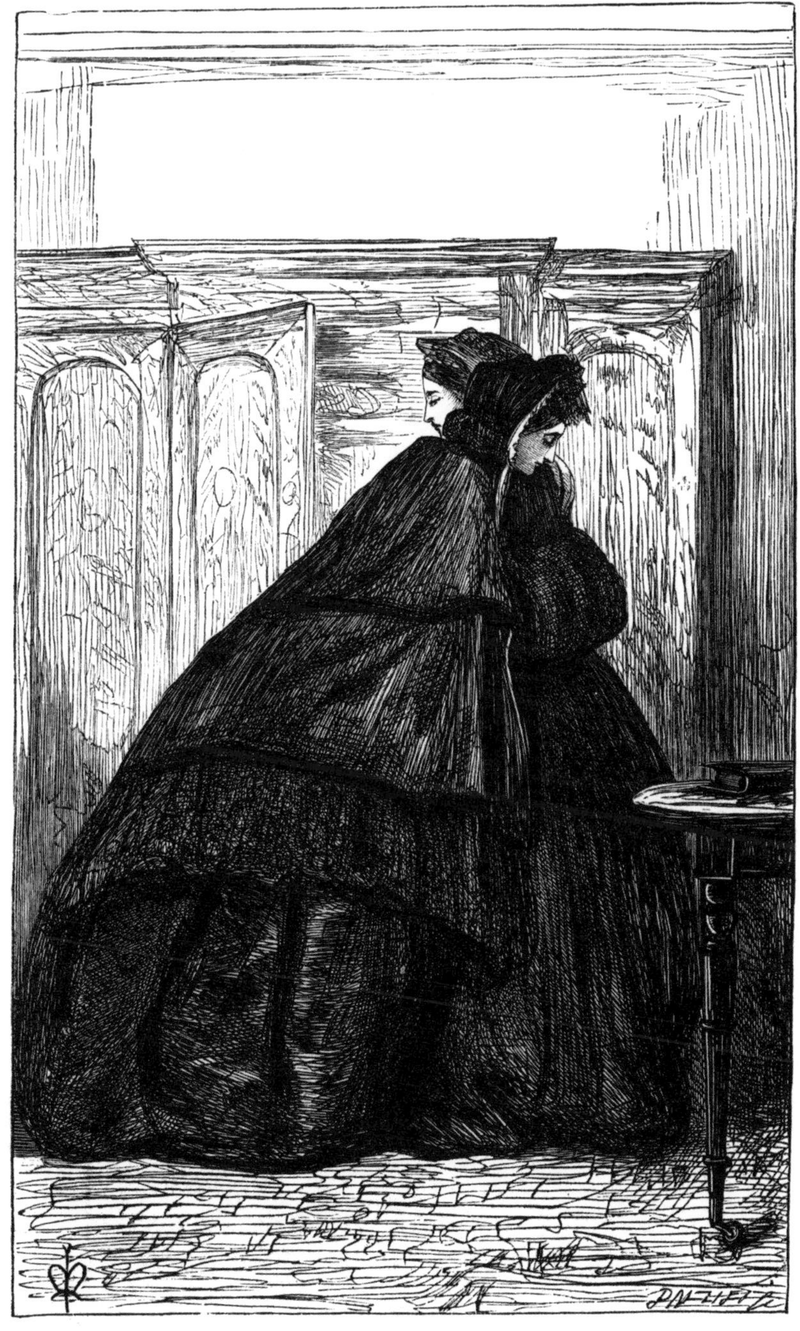

Millais's Collected Illustrations

Simon Cooke

JOHN EVERETT MILLAIS (1829–96) was one of the most versatile and accomplished artists of the Victorian age. He co-founded the Pre-Raphaelite Brotherhood (1848) in partnership with William Holman Hunt and D. G. Rossetti, and in the final year of his life he became the President of the Royal Academy. Millais's contribution to Victorian painting was significant, but he was also one of the most influential illustrators of his time. Instrumental in the development of the poetic-realist style known as 'The Sixties',[1] which was a version of Pre-Raphaelitism, he produced some hundreds of wood-engraved designs for literary texts in periodicals and books, in volumes of poetry, in novels, and in works for children.

Millais's Collected Illustrations was issued by the publisher Alexander Strahan as a showcase for these diverse images. Strahan's aim was to capitalize on Millais's popularity, repackaging pre-published material in the form of an attractive Christmas gift-book. It was issued in December 1865 and post-dated 1866 so it could be sold as a new book in that year as well, and it retailed at 16 shillings. This was expensive for the time, and Strahan —who probably made the selection without consulting with Millais—intended the album to appeal to a middle-class audience of buyers who were interested in art or imagined themselves to be connoisseurs. Tellingly, it was not intended for readers: as we can see, the illustrations are divorced from their texts, no texts are reproduced, and the images are presented as autonomous artworks. This approach was unusual at the time, though the idea of publishing his work in the form of an album was generally met with approval. Writing in *The Times*, for example, one critic observed that 'Mr Millais has qualities [that] give his illustrations independence of the text in which they appear ... [they] are works of art that need no letterpress—they speak for themselves and have an interest in themselves.'[2] Others were less approving —*The Bookseller* took the contrary view that the illustrations were diminished by being taken out of their textual framing—but most agreed, as noted in *The Westminster Review*,[3] that anyone 'who cares' for the 'progress of art' should 'study this volume'.[4]

So what, exactly, did *Millais's Collected Illustrations* offer to the original audience, and what does it offer us as viewers of the twenty-first century as we look through the pages of the current edition? Contemporary reviewers speak of the illustrations' 'power'[5] and 'sense of life,' the work of a 'poet,'[6] but these generalizations do little to characterize Millais's particular strengths. Rather, Strahan's volume can be seen as a skilful selection which presents various aspects of the artist's complex achievement as a 'poetic' practitioner who worked in diverse idioms, explored a variety of themes, and was often experimental in his approach to 'drawing on wood'.

Foremost among Millais's subjects is domestic life and the manners of the middle-classes. *Collected Illustrations* contains several scenes from Trollope's *Orley Farm* (1862), and each exemplifies the artist's capacity to represent 'modern' life in a way that celebrates the value of the ordinary. Like Trollope, Millais makes the mundane seem interesting: clothes are carefully specified, the home-settings are evocative, and the characters, consumed in their small dramas, move between conversations and moments of reverie. 'Lady Stavely interrupting her son and Sophie Farnwal' (no. 49) typifies the illustrator's ability to represent the intimate spaces of home as the mother unintentionally intrudes into a private conversation: the courtship is seen as her ladyship enters, dressed in a large crinoline, and the whole drama is framed by the prosaic details of an opening door, a patterned carpet and a half-glimpsed outline of a piece of elaborate furniture. Such small events are given prominence as part of a montage of bourgeois life that ranges from this uncovering of secrets to the joyous blind man's bluff on Christmas day (no. 62), which is shown as a vigorous mêlée of figures.

These scenes would have appealed to the original audiences of Strahan's volume, just as they did when they first appeared in the pages of Trollope's novel. In an age of facts and common sense, viewers were impressed by art which could see 'life … in commonplace things.'[7] Likewise, for the modern audience Millais tells us much about the character of Victorian society, its rituals, its manners, its 'look', its trappings, and—ultimately—its similarity to our own, 'modern' life.

At the same time, the *Collected Illustrations* exhibits Millais's talent as a chronicler of the past, the historical, the biblical, and the mythical. A great practitioner of the Victorian everyday, he is shown to be equally adept at representing the drama of 'The Ten Virgins' from *The Parables* (no. 54), 'The Finding of Moses' (1), the martyrdom of Margaret Wilson (no. 3) and 'Mary Queen of Scots at Buxton' (no. 14). These subjects are treated with the same intensity as those drawn from contemporary life; in the words of Paul Goldman, Millais was 'something of a chameleon'[8] who could shift idiom to suit a text while producing images that stand on their own as evocations of differing times and varying atmospheres. Mindful of the diverse interests of his audience, with some admiring Millais's modernity and some his historical pieces, Strahan was careful to include something for every taste.

Yet Millais's work was generally admired for what might be called his core characteristics. He was centrally concerned with psychological drama, the workings of introspection, and the dynamics of relationships. These themes underpin his approach whatever the subject, and to make sense of them he employs a number of stylistic devices, each of which can be studied in the pages of the *Collected Illustrations.*

Millais's domestic subjects are in the journalistic manner to suggest their immediacy, but he often manipulates styles which are diametrically opposed to each other, varying between a loose sketchiness and a dense blocking of the image. The first of these is associated with the historical illustrations, and conveys something of the dreaminess of the past, although Millais especially applies it to the representation of suffering, as in his image of Margaret Wilson's martyrdom, tied to a post and waiting for the sea to come in (no. 3). In this design the light, febrile lines suggest her anguish, as if the world is coming apart as she anticipates her death, with her hair blowing helplessly in the wind. It is a raw, visceral scene. Millais is similarly concerned with a sort of Gothic moodiness, using chiaroscuro and nocturnes to create eerie effects. A prime example of this approach is 'Cleopatra' (no. 63) from the famous edition of poems known as the *Moxon Tennyson* (1857), in which he shows the character's face emerging from the gloom as she points to her breast in anticipation of the asp's bite; another, equally atmospheric, is the 'Wind is blowing in turret and tree' from Tennyson's 'The Sisters' (1857). There are no figures in this design and only presents as a stark opposition of black architecture and the moon as it rises behind swirling trees (no. 7). In its original setting the image illustrates a place of suicide, but here it acts to evoke a Poe-like menace.

All of these evocative designs have considerable resonance. Time is arrested and we are compelled to contemplate moments of special significance. At the heart of Millais's psychological approach, however, is the 'significant gesture'—the use of a loaded expression or an intimate interaction between two characters, his usual dramatic unit.[9] The *Collected Illustrations* contains some of the best of these moving illustrations, with a special emphasis on female suffering. We have, for instance, Lady Mason's abstracted gaze as she realizes she must face up to her wrongdoing (having falsified a will) in images from *Orley Farm* (nos. 24, 77, 80). But equally important are love and romance, with many of the characters being engaged in passionate embraces, kissing, holding hands or looking mournfully at the beloved (nos. 4, 33, 48, 70, 78): sometimes the emotion is positive, and sometimes it is a matter of loss, and two illustrations exemplify Millais's capacity to convey the extremes. In 'Love'—perhaps his most famous design, lifted from *Poets of the Nineteenth Century* (1857)—he shows a couple enmeshed in each other's arms; their faces are not shown, and the emotional charge is entirely invested in their mutuality (no. 72). By contrast, in 'Bitterly weeping he turned away' (no. 9), the artist uses gesture to suggest the male character's grief, having lost his beloved, as he looks away and holds hands with his comforter. The illustration was taken from Tennyson's *Poems* (1857) and visualizes the anguish of Edward Gray; here, though, it is a universal sign of the psychological effects of bereavement, with the blankness of the background further acting to suggest the character's inner emptiness. Such powerful emotionalism, or 'deep sincerity,'[10] is typical of the artist's work and still speaks to us in the twenty-first century.

In short, *Millais's Collected Illustrations* is a representative medley which embodies the most characteristic ingredients of the artist's designs on wood. Of course, not everyone agreed with the selection, with some contemporary critics calling it 'very miscellaneous'[11] and marred by some 'careless'[12] drawing, even if, as noted earlier, most regarded the book as a great success. What Millais thought of it is unknown—though he must surely have appreciated the status accorded to his work in black and white as he consolidated his reputation as one of the outstanding painters of his age. At the very least, he must have viewed it as another form of promotion which kept him in the public eye by taking his art into the intimate spaces of home.

The power of the work was accentuated, moreover, by its packaging as a Christmas gift book: issued in a quarto (album sized) format, and bound in green cloth with gilt titling, its pages also had gilt edges. The effect, as in all such books, was one of luxuriousness, making it into a splendid visual artefact that would create a significant impact when it was unwrapped on Christmas morning. Most importantly of all, the illustrations were printed, impressively, as prints with broad margins, and were better presented than when they first appeared; the paper used in the *Illustrations* was of much higher quality than that used in the original books and periodicals, and the printing of the images is to a superior standard. It is not clear if Strahan made use of the original woodblocks rather than electrotypes (metal impressions taken from woodblocks), but we can certainly say, as Gleeson White points out, that 'the blocks have received more careful printing than that allowed by the exigencies of their ordinary publication.'[13]

In the absence of any financial records, we can assume that the book was a lucrative success for the publisher, whose only costs apart from the printing and binding would have been the payment for some of the blocks from Chapman and Hall (*Orley Farm*), Bradbury and Evans (*Once a Week*) and the other publishers of the work contained in the album; he already published *Good Words* and had ownership of Millais's illustrations for that periodical. He was under no obligation, it should be stressed, to pay Millais anything for the reproduction of his images, and we have no evidence that the illustrator benefited financially. Once an artist had produced work for a publisher the fee paid for each cut—on average between £15 and £20—included the copyright, and thereafter the publisher could exploit the image as he wished. Low in cost and high in appeal, the *Illustrations* was in many ways an ideal publication from Strahan's point of view. Indeed, at least one other publisher saw the opportunities in re-issuing previously issued designs in the same, textless format as Strahan's book. George Smith of Smith, Elder republished Leighton's illustrations in a deluxe issue of *Twenty-Five Illustrations by Frederick Leighton Designed for The Cornhill Magazine* (1867), and followed this up with *Twenty-Seven Illustrations by Frederick Walker* (1867).

However, it is only *Millais's Collected Illustrations* that still appeals as an anthology of designs, insisting on the artist's enduring interest as a chronicler of deep feeling and dazzling skill. In the words of Gleeson White (1897), the book is 'representative [of Millais's art] and full of superb work' and 'should be the blue riband of every collector.'[14] The present edition gives us a vivid sense of that original work and allows us, as modern observers, to look afresh.

NOTES

1. For discussion of this period, see: Forrest Reid, *Illustrators of the Sixties* (London: Faber & Dwyer, 1928); Paul Goldman, *Victorian Illustrated Books, 1850–1870: the Heyday of Wood Engraving* (London: British Museum, 1994); Simon Cooke, *Illustrated Periodicals of the 1860s* (London: British Museum, 2010)

2. Extract from an advertisement from *The Times* review (11 December 1865), in *The Athenaeum* (28 April 1865), p. 576

3. 'Millais's Collected Illustrations', *The Bookseller* (12 December 12), p. 820

4. 'Belles Lettres', *The Westminster Review* (January–April 1866), p. 596

5. *The Athenaeum* (28 April 28), p. 576

6. 'Gift Books', *The Examiner* (23 December 1865), p. 810

7. Ibid.

8. Paul Goldman, *Victorian Illustration: The Pre-Raphaelites, the Idyllic School and the High Victorians* (Aldershot: Scolar, 1996), p. 4

9. See Simon Cooke, 'John Everett Millais as an Illustrator – Significant Gesture, Expressive Line, and Emblematic Detail,' at The Victorian Web: https://victorianweb.org/art/illustration/millais/cooke.html

10. Paul Goldman, *John Everett Millais: Illustrator and Narrator* (Aldershot: Lund Humphries, 2004), p. 8

11. 'Belles Lettres', *Westminster Review*, p. 596

12. 'Millais's Collected Illustrations', *London Quarterly Review* 26 (1866), p. 254

13. Gleeson White, *English Illustration: The Sixties, 1855–70* (London: Constable, 1897), p. 131

14. Ibid.

More illustration from Pallas Athene

THE FOLLIES

by Francisco de Goya
24 black-and-white illustrations
ISBN 978 1 84368 255 4

Goya's last set of etchings were made between 1815 and 1824, the dark years after the fall of Napoleon, when the artist was living in his farm, the House of the Deaf Man. Enigmatic and sinister, the etchings were not published until long after Goya's death. Variously known as 'The Proverbs', 'The Dreams', or, most often, *Los Disparates*, 'The Follies', they are some of the most compelling images in Western art and their technical virtuosity is second to none.

ELEGIES OF LOVE

by Ovid, illustrated by Auguste Rodin
31 black-and-white illustrations
ISBN 978 1 84368 163 2

These woodcut illustrations to Rodin's favourite poems, the only printed versions of Rodin's work to receive his full approval, were taken from the astonishingly free and improvisatory life drawings the sculptor made in his later years.

Privately published in 1939 in a strictly limited edition, these 31 beautiful images are very rarely seen. They are paired here with Christopher Marlowe's glittering translation, which was ceremonially burnt by the Archbishop of Canterbury in 1599.

More illustration from Pallas Athene

IN THE BEGINNING
by Edward Burne-Jones
25 black-and-white illustrations
ISBN 978 1 84368 088 8

A series of designs to illustrate the first chapters of Genesis, and intended to have been part of a Kelmscott Bible, these woodcuts were left unpublished at Burne-Jones's death and were prepared for printing by his widow Georgiana. Burne-Jones's peerless sense of design is seen at its purest in these beautiful images; and the intensely careful balance of illustration and text makes this an epitome of the Kelmscott style.

THE OSLO SKETCHBOOK OF 1807
by Caspar David Friedrich
24 colour illustrations
ISBN 978 1 84368 274 5

Half of Friedrich's surviving drawings come from the sketchbooks that he compiled on journeys on the Baltic coast or in the Bohemian woods, and which he referred to during the whole of his career. A handful of these sketchbooks survive intact. The one known as the Oslo Sketchbook of 1807 was used for just two months, from April to June of that year. Its 24 drawings record, with almost hallucinatory simplicity and clarity, trees that Friedrich would use in his paintings for years to come.

Illustrated books by William Blake

THE GATES OF PARADISE
22 black-and-white illustrations
ISBN 978 1 84368 188 5

In this little book for children, first made in 1793, Blake charted the course of human life and experience in eighteen enigmatic emblems. Twenty-five years later, he revisited the book, adding three plates of explication and some captions. It remains one of his most accessible, yet disconcerting works.

THENOT AND COLINET
17 black-and-white illustrations
ISBN 978 1 84368 192 2

Blake's only wood engravings, made near the end of his life for a school edition of Virgil, are among his most lyrical and enduringly influential creations. This is the first time they have been published in book form, with the poetry that they illustrate.

Visions of little dells, and nooks, and corners
of Paradise; models of the exquisitest
intense pitch of poetry
Samuel Palmer

Illustrated books by William Blake

L'ALLEGRO E IL PENSEROSO
12 colour illustrations
ISBN 978 1 84368 189 2

Blake engaged with the legacy of Milton all his life. These watercolours, made around 1816-20 to illustrate the most perfect of Milton's shorter poems, are some of the finest of all the painter's works.

Milton lov'd me in childhood
& shew'd me his face
William Blake

ILLUSTRATIONS OF THE BOOK OF JOB
23 black-and-white illustrations
ISBN 978 1 84368 187 8

William Blake's last masterpiece of printmaking, commissioned by the painter John Linnell, and based on watercolours Blake had made around 1805. Three hundred copies were printed in 1826, and they earned Blake high recognition from fellow artists.

Of the highest rank in certain characters of
imagination and expression; ...in expressing
conditions of glaring and flickering light,
Blake is greater than Rembrandt
John Ruskin

Also from Pallas Athene

MILLAIS: A SKETCH by M. H. Spielmann
together with the artist's
THOUGHTS ON OUR ART OF TODAY
33 colour illustrations
ISBN 978 1 84368 034 5

This richly illustrated volume is the first republication of Millais's only finished work of art criticism, the pithy *Thoughts on our Art of Today*, paired with the hugely engaging 'Sketch' by the important critic Marion Spielmann, which gives both a warm and personal picture of the man and a level-headed evaluation of the qualities, and defects, of his work as they appeared to contemporaries.

MARRIAGE OF INCONVENIENCE
by Robert Brownell
600 pages with 55 illustrations
ISBN 978 1 84368 096 3

What really happened in the most scandalous love triangle of the nineteenth century? Was it all about impotence and pubic hair? Or was it about money, power and freedom? If so, whose? What possibilities were there for these young people caught in a world racked by social, financial and political turmoil? And whose interests were helped by turning an intensely private tragedy into a national scandal?

Based on newly uncovered documents, Robert Brownell's reappraisal of the relationship of Ruskin, Millais and Effie Gray has been widely acclaimed.